home sweet quilt

FRESH, EASY QUILT PATTERNS FROM JILLILY STUDIO

JILL FINLEY

Martingale
Create with Confidence

Home Sweet Quilt:
Fresh, Easy Quilt Patterns from Jillily Studio
© 2012 by Jill Finley

Martingale®
19021 120th Ave. NE, Ste. 102
Bothell, WA 98011-9511 USA
ShopMartingale.com

Printed in China
17 16 15 14 13 12   8 7 6 5 4 3 2 1

Library of Congress Cataloging-in-Publication Data is available upon request.

ISBN: 978-1-60468-086-7

Thank you to Karen Burns and Joan Beade for the use of their picture-perfect houses for the photo shoot.

Mission Statement

Dedicated to providing quality products and service to inspire creativity.

CREDITS

President & CEO: Tom Wierzbicki
Editor in Chief: Mary V. Green
Design Director: Paula Schlosser
Managing Editor: Karen Costello Soltys
Technical Editor: Laurie Baker
Copy Editor: Marcy Heffernan
Production Manager: Regina Girard
Illustrator: Missy Shepler
Cover & Text Designer: Adrienne Smitke
Photographer: Brent Kane

CONTENTS

INTRODUCTION

Nothing else quite matches the texture, warmth, and color that fabric brings to a space. Add to that the joy and satisfaction you feel when you create something beautiful. Quilts made especially for your home are the perfect ingredient in a successful design plan. They personalize and add character and charm to each room. This book will walk you through a quilter's home, decorating each area as you go with delightful designs.

When I started Jillily Studio, my goal was to create and share fresh quilt designs that weren't tired and out of style but still had an element of tradition. I wanted my designs to be at home in any setting, but most of all, I wanted to use them in *my* home. They're much more than blankets or bed coverings. They're the pop of color, the unexpected texture, or the softening elements of each room.

My handcrafted quilts reflect the love I have for the people around me. They share warmth with my family and guests and just make me smile. I hope you'll enjoy the same pleasures as you make some of the projects in this book to grace your home.

Happy quilting!

A FEW BASICS

The patterns in this book are written for the quilter who has a basic working knowledge of cutting and piecing. Some of the projects are pretty simple, and some are a little more complex. In this section, I'll share some quilting know-how that will help you create successful projects. After all, we all want successful projects, don't we? If you learn anything helpful here, pass it on!

FINDING FABRICS

Recently, as I was running late, I tried to explain to my daughter that I'd been "stuck in traffic," but it came out "stuck in fabric." We had a good laugh, but we both knew that it was the truth.

Have you ever been stuck in fabric? Sometimes it's overwhelming to pick all the fabrics needed for one project. There are so many wonderful choices at our quilt shops today, and fabric is readily available online as well. How do you get the right combination? Well, my advice is to go with what you love, and follow these guidelines to make it work:

- Always use good-quality 100% cotton quilting fabrics. There is a big difference between the goods you get at a big-box store as compared to your local quilt shop. You may even find similar prints, but the thread count and yarn strength will be much higher at a quilt shop.

When you're putting many hours of work into your quilt, you want your fabrics to be high quality.

- Use more than one fabric of each color. In other words, if your design needs a red fabric, use several different reds. Multiple fabrics add a lot of interest and depth—plus they make the quilt more fun to work on.

- Make sure your fabric choices have a variety of *scale* (size of design), *style* (type of design), and *visual texture*.

- Try not to only use fabrics from the same fabric line. Although they're beautiful and designed to go together, your finished quilt will tend to look "flat." That's because the fabrics are by the same designer and consequently have the same style and tone. Choose a few you love from one line and go on a hunt to find other fabrics that complement your selections and make them more interesting. This trick alone will make your creation unique and reflect *your* style.

- When you introduce a new color or fabric into your design, use it in more than one place so it looks like it belongs there. For example, if you get to the outside border and decide to use a print or color that doesn't relate to the rest of the quilt, it will look like you couldn't find anything to match, or that you ran out of fabric. However, if you use that same fabric somewhere else in the quilt, it will "belong."

- Lastly, audition your selections. Before you make a purchase, check the fabric in good light and from a distance as well as up close. Sometimes, in the store what you think will work doesn't actually work when you get home. (*Oh, darn, I need more fabric!*) Do a final audition on your design wall. Hang a piece of each fabric and step back. I like to look at the fabrics through a reducing lens, such as a peephole viewer or a camera lens, for a better perspective. Sometimes just leaving the room and coming back later with fresh eyes helps.

WORKING WITH WOOL

Two of the projects in this book use wool. One is an all-wool table runner, "Patio Tiles" (page 37), and the other is a pieced cotton wall hanging with wool appliqué titled "Overture" (page 25). You can make either of these projects using all cotton if you choose, but if you do, make sure that when you cut out the appliqué pieces, you add seam allowances so you can turn under the edges as described in "Appliqué the Jillily Way" on page 10. Using wool has many advantages, mainly that you don't have to turn under the edges on your appliqués—and of course the rich color and depth that wool brings to a project can't be matched!

Quilters don't usually buy wool yardage; instead they buy cut pieces, which are normally already felted. If you buy yardage, you can felt it yourself, but you'll need extra to allow for shrinkage. In this book, when a project calls for wool, I list the size of *felted wool* that the project requires. I frequently use scraps from my cupboard or cut up old woolen garments.

Felting wool makes the fabric denser and thicker, and it won't fray as easily. It adds a nice "chunky" dimension to your projects. You can felt your wool pieces easily by simply washing them in hot water with detergent or soap. You can do this in your washing machine or by hand in your sink. Just make sure that you agitate the fabric enough to get the little wool fibers to mat together, creating felt. The soap also adds to the process by making the fibers slip over each other. I use dish detergent when I felt fabric by hand. Use very hot water to encourage shrinkage, bringing the fibers even closer together. When you're done washing the fabric, wring it out or spin the water out, and then dry it in a hot dryer. Press the felted fabric with a hot steam iron.

ATTACHING BORDERS

The border sizes given in the instructions for each quilt are mathematically correct. *If* your piecing was perfect, and *if* your fabric didn't stretch, and *if* your machine didn't feed the fabrics at different rates, well, then it would work perfectly! But that's a lot of *ifs*. So, it's wise to measure your quilt top through the vertical center and the horizontal center to make sure you're in the ballpark. If there's a discrepancy greater than ½" between your measurements and those in the project instructions, change your border size to match your quilt top before you cut.

I like to use the mathematically correct sizes, because I check my block sizes as I go, and this keeps my quilt square. The block or section sizes are given in my instructions. Use these measurements to make sure everything fits together perfectly.

CHOOSING THE QUILTING ELEMENTS

When you get to the end of almost any quilt pattern, the instructions tell you to layer the quilt with batting and backing and quilt as desired. While it can be frustrating not to have specifics, quilting is a personal preference, and the type of batting you choose, as well as the quilting design, can give a quilt its unique personality.

Many of us take our quilt tops to a long-arm quilter to be finished and rely on her or him to make the decisions. Personally, I want to be the one to make those decisions, so I usually take my own batting, and I always give my quilter some idea for a quilting design. Share your vision with your quilter, and you can create a work of art together!

The type of batting you choose will affect the drape, weight, and look of your quilt. Choose wisely! My favorite brand of batting is Quilter's Dream. All of the quilts featured in this book have been quilted with Quilter's Dream batting, and I've used every type from 100% cotton to wool and blends. I just love the quality and variety I can get from this brand. If you want to achieve the same look as my quilts, I've mentioned the type of batting I used in the instructions for each project.

As for the quilting design, whether you quilt the project yourself or enlist the services of a long-arm quilter, follow these points to get a finished quilt you'll be proud of:

- Never quilt over the top of an appliqué. If you quilt around it, the motifs will puff out and be more accentuated. You can treat any pieced element the same way—quilt the background around it tightly and the piecing will stand out.
- Add quilting designs in borders and open spaces that echo the prints in the fabric or the pieced elements.
- Soften pieced shapes with curved quilting lines.
- Use a variety of scale in the quilting designs so that they will stand out by adding contrast.

BINDING

I like to think of binding as the frame around the quilt. It's the perfect little outline to finish off the project. Here's how I create perfect bindings.

1. Cut your binding strips 2¼" wide. This ensures that as the binding folds around the raw edges of the quilt, it will be full and not flat. Also, if you have a pieced border, you could cut off your points if the binding is too wide.

2. Sew together your binding strips using a diagonal seam. Trim the excess fabric and press the seam allowances open to reduce bulk. Fold the binding in half lengthwise, wrong sides together, and press.

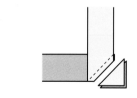

3. Beginning along one side of the quilt top, not at a corner, lay the binding on the quilt top, aligning the raw edges. Leaving about 10" of binding unattached, begin sewing the binding using a generous ¼" seam allowance. Use a walking foot to sew on your binding—there are so many layers of fabric and batting and binding, something is sure to shift and you'll end up with puckers or wobbly edges. If you don't have a walking foot, pin through all of the layers at least every 3". Stop sewing ¼" from the first corner and backstitch. Clip the thread and remove the quilt from under the presser foot.

4. Turn your quilt to continue down the next side. Fold the binding away from you to create a 45° angle at the corner. Then fold the binding back down onto itself to square the corner, keeping the corner angle intact. Align the quilt and binding raw edges. Start stitching from the fold and continue to the next corner. Because there's extra bulk at the corners, I make my seam allowance just slightly narrower at the corners to allow the fabric to fold over evenly.

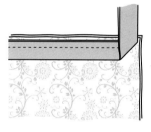

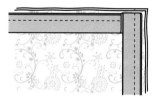

5. Repeat step 4 at each corner. When you're approximately 10" from your starting point, stop and backstitch. Fold the loose tails at the beginning and ending of the binding away from each other at a 90° angle with the folds butted together. Press the folds to mark the diagonal angles. Pull the binding strips away from the quilt, open up the folds, and sew them together along the marked diagonal seam, keeping them at right angles to each other. Trim the seam allowances to ¼" and press them open. Now finish sewing the binding to the quilt.

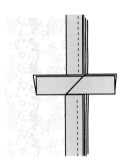

6. Turn your folded binding edge to the back of the quilt and hand stitch it in place (see "Jill's Favorite Hand-Stitching Supplies" at right.

Jill's Favorite Hand-Stitching Supplies

Anytime I have to hand stitch, whether it's stitching the binding to the back of the quilt or stitching appliqués in place, these are the supplies I have in my little kit.

- Aurifil thread: This is a good-quality long-staple Egyptian cotton thread. The 50 weight is ideal for hand stitching, because it's fine yet strong and very smooth.

- Bohin #11 appliqué needles: These needles are thin and sharp. The eye is sanded, creating a smooth surface for the thread to pass through, which leads to fewer snags.

- Jillily Studio Poke-A-Dots: Stick one of these little dots to the pad of the finger you use to push the needle through the fabric. Poke-A-Dots are like a thimble, but much more lightweight and smaller. The textured surface keeps the needle from slipping and protects your finger, making for easy, quick needle pushing. The little tin they come in can hold your needles and threads too. Sometimes if I need to take along many different thread colors, I wind thread onto bobbins so I can fit more in the tin. Then I have everything I need in one little package!

- Embroidery scissors

APPLIQUÉ *the* JILLILY WAY

Here's what I use to prepare my appliqués: an iron, freezer paper, spray starch, a small stencil brush, a tailor's awl, Jillily Studio Appli-Glue, and dressmaker's shears.

I find it hard not to add "just a little bit" of appliqué to every quilt. The sharp, straight lines of piecing are complemented so well by the graceful curves and soft patterns of appliqué. Many quilters are afraid to try it, but once you do, you'll realize how much it can add to your creations, and it isn't too difficult. This method makes appliqué easy for anyone to do. Give it a try and before you know it, you'll be beautifying everything around you with "just a little bit."

PREPARING THE APPLIQUÉ PIECES

Gather the supplies you need to prepare your appliqué pieces, and then follow the steps to get your appliqués ready.

1. Tear off four pieces of freezer paper that are large enough to trace all of the patterns onto.

2. Trace one of each appliqué pattern given for the project onto the dull side of one piece of freezer paper. Transfer the solid and dotted lines and reverse shapes if specified.

3. With the shiny sides down and the traced patterns on top, layer all four pieces of freezer paper. Press the papers together with a hot iron so that they fuse together.

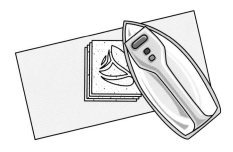

4. Cut out each pattern on the solid lines and just outside of the dotted lines (so you can see where they are) to make a template.

5. Place each template shiny side down on the wrong side of the appropriate fabric; press with a hot iron to stick the template to the fabric.

6. Cut around each template, leaving a scant ¼" seam allowance beyond the solid lines and cutting directly along the edges that have dotted lines. The edges with dotted lines will be under another piece and don't need a seam allowance.

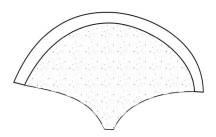

7. Clip inside curves if needed, about ⅛" into the seam allowance. A sharp inside point, like on the top of a heart shape, will need to be clipped all the way to the template, *but*, before you clip, put a tiny drop of a no-fray product on the fabric where you will need to cut. This will prevent the fabric from unraveling.

8. Spray some starch or sizing into a small cup. It will foam up and then liquefy. Use a small stencil brush to "paint" the seam allowance of one of the appliqué pieces with the liquid starch.

9. Place the appliqué piece on your ironing board. Use a tailor's awl or stiletto to hold the appliqué piece so you don't get burned. With a hot, dry iron, press the wet seam allowance over the freezer-paper template, keeping the iron on the seam allowance until it's dry. Remember not to turn under edges along dotted lines.

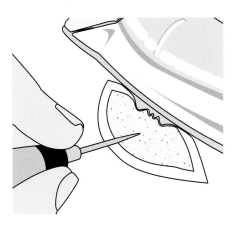

If you're working with a shape that has a sharp point, such as at the tip of a leaf, press one side of the leaf and then the other side of the leaf, leaving the extra fabric, or "flag," sticking out on the end. Do *not* trim off the flag. You'll tuck the extra fabric under with your needle as you stitch the appliqué in place.

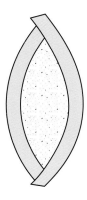

10. Let the piece cool, and then remove the freezer-paper template. The seam allowances will remain crisply turned under and stay in place after you remove the template. Reuse the freezer-paper template to make as many pieces of that shape as needed for the project. The template can be used until it no longer sticks to the fabric.

11. Repeat steps 8–10 with the remaining templates.

PREPARING BIAS TAPE

I create stems and vines from bias tape that I've made using a bias-tape maker. Bias-tape makers come in several sizes.

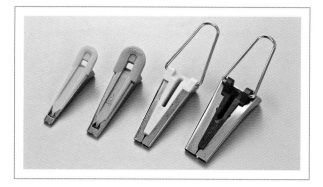

Bias-tape makers in sizes from ¼" to ¾"

1. Cut fabric strips on the bias—at a 45° angle to the lengthwise and crosswise grain. The width of the cut strips depends on the desired finished width of your bias strip. Cut the strips twice the finished width plus ⅛". For example, if you want a ¼"-wide finished bias strip, cut a ⅝"-wide bias strip (¼ x 2 = ½ + ⅛ = ⅝). The additional ⅛" ensures there'll be enough fabric to turn under the edges nicely. Join strips if needed to achieve the necessary length. All of the patterns in this book give you the size strip to cut and the size bias-tape maker to use.

2. Lightly spray starch or sizing onto the strip *before* you pass it through the bias-tape maker, but don't iron it yet. If you apply the starch or sizing after you make the strip, the moisture will undo the pressed folds. This step is important because it helps hold the creases in the strip and makes the bias tape very crisp and easy to work with. It also helps the vine or stem keep its shape when you press it into a curve.

3. Feed the fabric strip into the bias-tape maker with the wrong side facing up toward the top of the bias-tape maker.

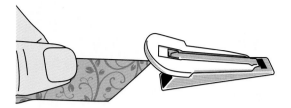

4. Turn the bias-tape maker over, insert a pin or awl tip through the slot on the bottom, and slide the fabric out the other end of the bias-tape maker.

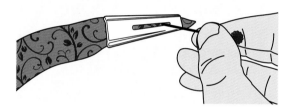

5. Now, turn the bias-tape maker back over so that the top is facing up. Pin the end of the fabric strip to your ironing surface to hold it in place. Slowly pull back on the bias-tape maker as you slide your iron along behind it. The edges of the fabric strip will come out folded, and the iron will press the folds flat.

6. Shape your finished bias tape into any curves you need using your iron. For this I like to use steam so that it reactivates the starch that's already in the fabric. Don't spray the bias tape with starch at this point or the moisture will undo the folds. To follow a pattern, trace it onto

a piece of paper and place it on your ironing surface. Put the prepared bias tape right side up on the pattern. Use a hot iron to form the bias tape into the shape of the pattern. You may have to make several passes with your iron to shape tight circles.

POSITIONING THE APPLIQUÉS

1. When you have all of your appliqué pieces prepared, refer to the appliqué placement guide given with the project to place the prepared appliqué pieces on the background fabric, starting from the bottom layer and working to the top.

2. Glue baste each appliqué in place with Jillily Studio Appli-Glue. Appli-Glue is a temporary basting glue and is safe to use on fabrics. It will not discolor or harm the fibers whether you wash the quilt or not. You can apply the glue to each appliqué before you position it or wait until all of the appliqués are placed on the background fabric. The bottle of this archival-quality glue has a long precision tip so you can reach under your pieces without disturbing their placement to glue them down. Don't use too much glue, just a tiny dot every ½" to 1" along the seam allowance of the appliqué piece. I like to be sure the glue isn't too close to the folded edge of the appliqué so that I don't sew through it but that it's still on the seam allowance and doesn't come through to the right side of the fabric.

STITCHING THE APPLIQUÉS

At this point you're ready to stitch. You can stitch by hand or machine. I love to hand stitch, because it's so beautiful, and it makes your project portable. I can hand stitch while I'm spending time outside of my sewing room—perfect for waiting rooms and sporting events. However, sometimes there just isn't time to hand appliqué, or you may want a project to have a different look. For these occasions, I stitch my appliqué by machine, but I still prepare the pieces the same way so that I have no raw edges. Following are the instructions for hand and machine stitching.

Hand Stitching

Refer to "Jill's Favorite Hand-Stitching Supplies" on page 9 for the supplies you'll need. Select a thread color that matches the appliqué, not the background.

1. Thread your needle with a single strand of thread and knot one end.

2. Hold your appliqué project with the appliqué piece toward you and the edge that you're stitching on away from you. You'll be stitching from right to left if you're right-handed and from left to right if you're left-handed. If possible, start stitching along a straight or gently curved edge.

3. Stick a Poke-A-Dot on your "pushing" finger. This will allow you to maneuver your needle easily.

4. Bring the needle up from the wrong side to the right side through the background, coming out of the fold of the appliqué. Insert the needle back into the background a tiny bit under the appliqué edge and come back up about ⅛" away from the first stitch, coming out of the fold of the appliqué piece.

For appliqué shapes with outer points that have a flag of seam allowance sticking out, sew up to the point, using closely spaced stitches for the last ½" before the point. Put your needle in the very point of the appliqué piece, and tug on the thread gently to sharpen the point. Now use the tip of your needle to fold the flag under the appliqué and against the wall of stitching you just completed on the adjacent side. Stitch down the next side using closely spaced stitches for the first ½" beyond the point.

5. To end, pull the needle and thread through to the wrong side of the background fabric, run the needle under a thread of a stitch and then through the loop in the thread to knot it. Do this twice, and then run the thread between the background fabric and appliqué for about 2" and bring the needle out through the appliqué. Clip the thread close to the appliqué.

6. After all of the appliqué pieces have been stitched to the background, press the piece from the wrong side, if needed, on a soft pressing surface. Your pieces will be crisp and puff up a little as you quilt around them, and they'll have the look of beautiful needle-turned appliqué.

Machine Stitching

1. First, if you have any appliqué pieces with "flags" sticking out at the point, these need to be turned under. Use a needle or an awl to slide the flag under and glue baste it in place with Jillily Studio Appli-Glue.

2. Set your machine for a narrow (about ⅛"-wide) zigzag stitch. On my machine, I set the stitch length and width at 1. For your top thread, use monofilament in clear or smoke, depending on the color of your appliqué (use whichever one is less noticeable), or use matching cotton thread if you prefer. Turn your tension down so it doesn't stretch and pucker your work. Use cotton thread in your bobbin and a size 70 or 75 machine needle so that the holes it makes will be small.

3. Start with your needle down in the background right next to the appliqué piece. Zigzag onto your appliqué and then back into the background. Stitch around all the edges of your appliqués, including both sides of your stems and vines.

If you want a more decorative look, use a machine blanket stitch with either matching thread or contrasting thread. Straight stitching close to the edge of the appliqué pieces is also an option. Try it out before you use it on your prepared quilt top to see if you like the look. I used this method on the letters in "Berry Patch" on page 47.

FIRST IMPRESSIONS

From the front porch to the foyer, these quilts greet you and your guests as you first arrive. They add a cheerful, welcoming note to the front of your home. There won't be any doubt that a quilter lives here!

CROSSROADS

Finished quilt size: 54½" x 70½" • Finished block size: 8" x 8"

*Pieced and appliquéd by Jill Finley;
quilted by Tori Spencer*

Throw a cozy lap quilt over a seat on the front porch or inside the front door, and it instantly creates an inviting and warm space. This quilt is the perfect candidate because it's so colorful and textural. The lap-quilt size is just right, and the piecing lines intersect just like a community. Large yo-yos finish it off with a touch of whimsy.

MATERIALS

Yardage is based on 42"-wide fabric.

3 yards of green fabric for X blocks, setting blocks, and outer border

1⅛ yards of white print for inner border

⅝ yard *total* of assorted red fabrics for X blocks and yo-yos

⅝ yard *total* of assorted yellow fabrics for X blocks and yo-yos

½ yard *total* of assorted orange fabrics for X blocks and yo-yos

½ yard *total* of assorted pink fabrics for X blocks and yo-yos

⅝ yard of striped fabric for binding

3½ yards of fabric for backing

60" x 76" piece of batting

Jillily Studio Appli-Glue (optional)

CUTTING

From the green fabric, cut:

17 squares, 8½" x 8½"

18 squares, 4" x 4"; cut into quarters diagonally to yield 72 triangles

16 strips, 2½" x 42"; crosscut *9 of the strips* into 72 rectangles, 2½" x 4½"

6 strips, 1½" x 42"; crosscut into 144 squares, 1½" x 1½"

From the assorted red, yellow, orange, and pink fabrics, cut a *total* of 18 sets (5 red, 5 yellow, 4 orange, and 4 pink) with each set made up of:

4 squares, 2½" x 2½" (72 total)

4 squares, 1½" x 1½" (72 total)

1 strip, 1¼" x 16"; crosscut into:

    2 rectangles, 1¼" x 4" (36 total)

    1 rectangle, 1¼" x 8" (18 total)

Keep the pieces from each set together.

Continued on page 18.

From the remainder of the assorted red, yellow, orange, and pink fabrics, cut a *total* of:

35 circles using the yo-yo pattern on page 20 (11 red, 9 yellow, 8 orange, and 7 pink)

From the white print, cut:

6 strips, 5½" x 42"

From the striped fabric:

7 strips, 2¼" x 42"

MAKING THE BLOCKS

1. Working with one set of red pieces, sew a 1¼" x 4" rectangle between two green triangles as shown. Repeat to make a total of two units. Press the seam allowances toward the rectangles.

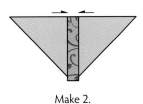

Make 2.

2. Sew the red 1¼" x 8" rectangle between the two units from step 1. Press the seam allowances toward the rectangle. Trim the block to 4½" x 4½". Make sure you keep the X centered in the square and going straight into each corner.

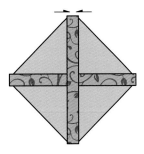

3. Sew green 1½" squares to adjacent sides of a red 1½" square. Press the seam allowances toward the green squares. Repeat with the three remaining red squares in the set to make a total of four units.

Make 4.

4. Place a unit from step 3 on top of a red 2½" square, right sides together. Sew diagonally from corner to corner as shown (you can mark the diagonal line if needed). Trim ¼" from the stitching line. Press the seam allowance toward the red triangle. Repeat to make a total of four corner squares.

Make 4.

5. Arrange the X unit from step 2, the four corner squares from step 4, and four green 2½" x 4½" rectangles into three horizontal rows. Sew the pieces in each row together. Press the seam allowances toward the rectangles. Sew the rows together. Press the seam allowances outward. The finished block should measure 8½" x 8½".

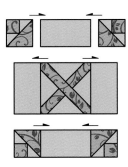 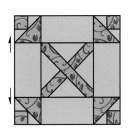

6. Repeat steps 1–5 with the remaining red, yellow, orange, and pink sets to make a total of 18 pieced blocks.

ASSEMBLING THE QUILT CENTER

1. Refer to the quilt assembly diagram on page 19 to lay out the pieced blocks and green 8½" squares in seven horizontal rows, alternating the blocks and squares in each row and from row to row. Randomly place the pieced blocks so the colors create a pleasing arrangement. When you're satisfied with the arrangement, sew the blocks in each row together. Press the seam allowances toward the green squares. Sew the rows together.

   Press the seam allowances in one direction. The quilt center should measure 40½" x 56½".

2. To make the yo-yos, select a 3½" fabric circle. Thread a hand-sewing needle with strong thread, but do not knot it. Leaving a thread tail at the beginning of your stitching, turn the circle's edge to the wrong side about ¼" and hand stitch it in place near the center of the seam allowance with running stitches that are about ¼" long. Continue working around the circle, turning under the edge and stitching it in place. When you've stitched completely around the circle, clip the thread, leaving another tail.

3. Pull on both ends of the hanging threads to gather the circle tight. Your circle will now look like a little pouch. Pull the gathers as tight as you can and tie the threads together in a knot, but do not clip the excess yet. Flatten out the little pouch, keeping all the gathers in the middle and spreading out the pleats evenly to make a yo-yo. Thread your needle with the hanging threads and carry them to the back of the yo-yo. Knot the threads on the back of the yo-yo, and then clip the excess threads.

4. Repeat steps 2 and 3 with the remaining 3½" circles to make a total of 35 yo-yos.
5. Use Jillily Studio Appli-Glue to glue baste a yo-yo to the center of each block and each green square on the quilt top. Hand stitch each yo-yo in place as you would an appliqué.

ADDING THE BORDERS

1. Join the white-print 5½" x 42" strips together end to end to make one long strip. Press the seam allowances in one direction. From the pieced strip, cut two 56½"-long strips and two 50½"-long strips.
2. Sew the 56½"-long strips to the sides of the quilt center. Press the seam allowances toward the border strips. Sew the 50½"-long strips to the top and bottom of the quilt center. Press the seam allowances toward the border strips.
3. Join the green 2½" x 42" strips together end to end to make one long strip. Press the seam allowances in one direction. From the pieced strip, cut two 66½"-long strips and two 54½"-long strips.
4. Sew the 66½"-long strips to the sides of the quilt top. Press the seam allowances toward the newly added border strips. Sew the 54½"-long strips to the top and bottom of the quilt top. Press the seam allowances toward the newly added border strips.

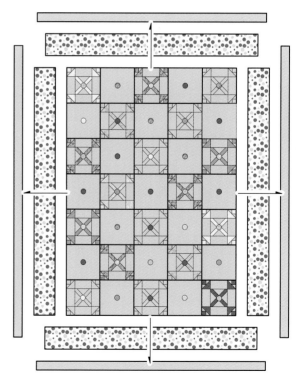

Quilt assembly

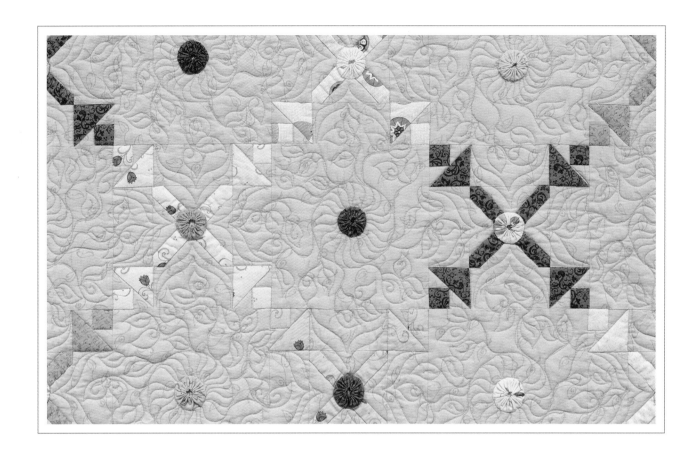

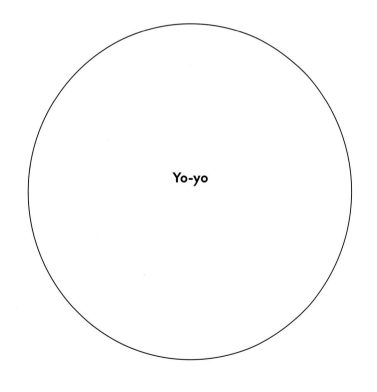

Yo-yo

FINISHING

1. Layer the quilt top with batting and backing. I used 100% cotton batting in this quilt.

2. Quilt as desired.

3. Bind the edges with the striped 2¼" x 42" strips.

HIGHWAYS *and* BYWAYS

Finished pillow size: 20" x 20" · Finished block size: 6" x 6"

Pieced by Jill Finley; quilted by Maika Christensen

A pair of throw pillows tossed on a patio bench are a welcoming sight to passers-by. These pillows are especially fun because you can vary the color placement to create different designs with the simple pieced blocks. Whip up a pair of cheerful pillows to enjoy in your outdoor space.

MATERIALS
Yardage is based on 42"-wide fabric.

For the Red Pillow
¼ yard of red print for blocks
⅛ yard *total* of 2 assorted green prints for blocks
⅛ yard *total* of 2 assorted yellow prints for blocks
¼ yard of yellow floral for inner border
⅛ yard of red herringbone print for flanged
    outer border

For the Yellow Pillow
⅓ yard of yellow print for blocks and flanged
    outer border
⅓ yard of green floral for blocks and inner border
⅛ yard of coral print for blocks

For **Each** *Pillow*
22" x 22" square of batting
¾ yard of muslin for pillow-front backing
⅔ yard of fabric for pillow back
18" x 18" pillow form

CUTTING
For the Red Pillow
From red print, cut:
4 squares, 6½" x 6½"; cut into quarters diagonally to
    yield 16 triangles

**From *each* of the 2 assorted green prints and 2
assorted yellow prints, cut:**
1 strip, 1½" x 24" (4 total); crosscut into:
    2 rectangles, 1½" x 6" (8 total)
    1 rectangle, 1½" x 12" (4 total)

From the yellow floral, cut:
2 strips, 3" x 42"; crosscut into:
    2 rectangles, 3" x 12½"
    2 rectangles, 3" x 17½"

Continued on page 23.

From the red herringbone print, cut:

2 strips, 2" x 42"; crosscut into:
    2 rectangles, 2" x 17½"
    2 rectangles, 2" x 20½"

For the Yellow Pillow

From the yellow print, cut:

4 squares, 6½" x 6½"; cut into quarters diagonally
    to yield 16 triangles
2 strips, 2" x 42"; crosscut into:
    2 rectangles, 2" x 17½"
    2 rectangles, 2" x 20½"

From the green floral, cut:

2 strips, 1½" x 42"; crosscut into 4 rectangles,
    1½" x 12"
2 strips, 3" x 42"; crosscut into:
    2 rectangles, 3" x 12½"
    2 rectangles, 3" x 17½"

From the coral print, cut:

2 strips, 1½" x 42"; crosscut into 8 rectangles,
    1½" x 6"

For Each Pillow

From the muslin, cut:

1 square, 22" x 22"

From the fabric for backing, cut:

1 square, 20½" x 20½"

MAKING THE BLOCKS

Instructions given are for the red pillow. To make the yellow pillow, use the same method, changing the color of the X strips as shown in the photo.

1. Sew a green 1½" x 6" rectangle between two red triangles as shown. Repeat to make a total of two units. Press the seam allowances toward the rectangles.

Make 2.

2. Sew the matching green 1½" x 12" rectangle between the two units from step 1. Press the seam allowances toward the rectangle. Trim the block to 6½" x 6½". Make sure you keep the X centered in the block and going straight into each corner.

3. Repeat steps 1 and 2 with the remaining green and yellow rectangles and red triangles to make a total of four X blocks.

ASSEMBLING THE PILLOW TOP

1. Arrange the X blocks into two horizontal rows of two blocks each as shown. Sew the blocks in each row together. Press the seam allowances toward the green blocks. Sew the rows together. Press the seam allowances in one direction. The pillow center should measure 12½" x 12½".

2. Refer to the pillow assembly diagram below to sew yellow floral 3" x 12½" rectangles to the top and bottom of the pillow center. Press the seam allowances toward the rectangles. Sew yellow floral 3" x 17½" rectangles to the sides of the pillow center. Press the seam allowances toward the rectangles.

3. Sew red herringbone 2" x 17½" rectangles to the top and bottom of the pillow top. Press the seam allowances toward the rectangles. Sew red herringbone 2" x 20½" rectangles to the sides of the pillow top. Press the seam allowances toward the rectangles. The pillow top should measure 20½" x 20½".

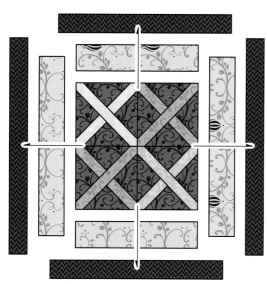

Pillow assembly

FINISHING

1. Layer the pillow front with batting and the muslin 22" square. Quilt as desired. I used cotton-blend batting. Trim the batting and backing even with the pillow-top edges.

2. Place the quilted pillow front on top of the backing fabric 20½" square, right sides together. Using a walking foot, stitch ¼" from the edges around the pillow, leaving a 12"-wide opening for turning. If you don't have a walking foot, pin all the edges securely, and then stitch with your all-purpose foot.

3. Turn the pillow cover to the right side through the opening. Leaving a 12"-wide opening that aligns with the outer 12"-wide opening, stitch around the pillow in the ditch between the red herringbone and yellow floral borders to make the border flange.

Stitch.

4. Insert the pillow form into the cover. (The actual pillow space for the form is less than 17" x 17"; the larger form makes the pillow nice and fluffy.) Compress the pillow form away from the side with the opening and pin through the pillow front and back layers, keeping the pillow form out of the way.

5. Turn in the ¼" seam allowances along the opening. Stitch in the ditch between the borders along the inner opening. Topstitch around the outer edge of the border flange. Remove the pins and fluff the pillow.

OVERTURE

Finished quilt size: 41½" x 41½" · Finished center block size: 21" x 21"

Pieced and appliquéd by Jill Finley; quilted by Virginia Gore

This cheery wall hanging will have your guests wanting to see more of the lovely quilts in your home. Using wool for the appliqué adds such rich color and texture. The small-scale piecing in the borders makes the large center medallion stand out and adds movement through the introduction of many colors and prints. You'll enjoy making this quilt as much as your guests will enjoy seeing it!

MATERIALS

Yardage is based on 42"-wide fabric.

1⅛ yards *total* of assorted cream prints for inner and outer border backgrounds

⅝ yard of cream print for center appliquéd-square background

⅝ yard *total* of assorted green prints for pieced inner and outer borders

½ yard of red-and-white print for setting triangles and binding

½ yard of red solid for middle border

¼ yard *total* of assorted red prints for pieced inner border

¼ yard of gold print for pieced inner border

12" x 12" square of dark-green felted wool for stem and leaf appliqués

4" x 10" piece of medium-red felted wool for flower and bud appliqués

4" x 10" piece of dark-red felted wool for flower and bud appliqués

4" x 6" piece of light-green felted wool for leaf and calyx appliqués

2" x 4" piece of gold felted wool for flower-center appliqué

2½ yards of fabric for backing

45" x 45" square of batting

Freezer paper

Jillily Studio Appli-Glue (optional)

Embroidery floss in red, green, and gold to match wool

Hand-sewing needles: size 7 embroidery and size 11 appliqué

Approximately 20 gold seed beads

CUTTING

Refer to "Appliqué the Jillily Way" on page 10 and use patterns A–M on page 30 to make templates for cutting the appliqué pieces.

From the cream print for the center appliquéd square, cut:
1 square, 15¾" x 15¾"

From the medium-red wool, cut:
1 *each* of A and C
2 of G

From the dark-red wool, cut:
1 *each* of B, D, H, and H reversed

From the 12" square of dark-green wool, cut:
1 bias strip, ½" x 16"
1 bias strip, ½" x 8"
1 bias strip, ½" x 5"
1 *each* of I, J, and K

From the light-green wool, cut:
2 of F
1 *each* of J, L, and M

From the gold wool, cut:
1 of E

From the red-and-white print, cut:
2 squares, 11½" x 11½"; cut in half diagonally to yield 4 setting triangles
5 strips, 2¼" x 42"

From the assorted cream prints, cut a *total* of:
6 strips, 3½" x 42"
64 squares, 2⅜" x 2⅜"; cut each square in half diagonally to yield 128 triangles
16 squares, 2½" x 2½"

From the assorted red prints, cut a *total* of:
4 strips, 1⅝" x 21"

From the gold print, cut:
2 strips, 1⅝" x 42"; crosscut into 4 strips, 1⅝" x 21"

From the assorted green prints, cut:
6 strips, 1½" x 42"
2 strips, 2⅝" x 42"; crosscut into 16 squares, 2⅝" x 2⅝"
4 squares, 4½" x 4½"

From the red solid, cut:
4 strips, 3½" x 42"; crosscut into:
2 strips, 3½" x 27½"
2 strips, 3½" x 33½"

MAKING THE CENTER BLOCK

1. Refer to "Working with Wool" on page 7, "Positioning the Appliqués" on page 13, and the placement diagram below to arrange the appliqués on the cream-print 15¾" square. Use the green-wool bias strips to create the stems, shaping them as shown and using an iron if needed to create the curves. The bias strips are longer than needed, so you'll need to trim them when you have the proper placement. Place the stems and the other appliqué pieces on the background square, and then glue baste them in place using Jillily Studio Appli-Glue.

Appliqué placement

2. With the size 7 embroidery needle, hand stitch each appliqué in place using a blanket stitch and three strands of matching embroidery floss. Use an appliqué needle and a doubled strand of matching all-purpose thread (or a single strand of 28-weight quilting thread) to hand stitch about 20 single seed beads to the flower center, spacing the beads about ½" apart.

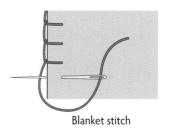

Blanket stitch

3. Trim the appliquéd block to 15⅜" square. Sew red-and-white print triangles to opposite sides of the appliquéd square, being careful not to stretch the bias edges. Press the seam allowances toward the triangles. Repeat on the remaining two sides of the square. The center block should measure 21½" x 21½".

PIECING AND ADDING THE BORDERS

1. Sew a gold 1⅝" x 21" strip to an assorted red strip along the long edges to make a strip set. Press the seam allowances toward the red strip. Repeat to make a total of four strip sets. Crosscut the strip sets into 32 segments, 1⅝" wide.

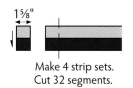

Make 4 strip sets.
Cut 32 segments.

2. Join two segments from step 1 as shown. Press the seam allowances in one direction. Repeat to make a total of 16 four-patch units. Trim each unit to 2⅝" x 2⅝", keeping the seams centered.

Make 1(

3. Fold each assorted cream-print triangle in half and finger-press a crease at the center of the long edge. Sew cream-print triangles to opposite sides of a four-patch unit, matching the creases to the seam lines. Press the seam allowances toward the triangles. Repeat on the remaining two sides of the unit. Repeat to make a total of 16 units. The units should measure 3½" x 3½".

Make 16.

4. Repeat step 3 to sew the remaining cream-print triangles to the assorted green 2⅝" squares. Make 16.

Make 16.

5. To make the inner side borders, refer to the quilt assembly diagram on page 29 or the photo on page 25 to alternately sew together four four-patch units from step 3 and three green units from step 4, rotating the four-patch units as shown. Press the seam allowances toward the green units. Repeat to make a total of two side borders, being aware that the four-patch units are rotated in different directions on each side of the quilt. The border strips should measure 3½" x 21½". Sew the borders to the sides of the center block. Press the seam allowances toward the center block.

6. Referring to step 5, sew four four-patch units and five green units together to make the top border. Repeat to make the bottom border, again being careful to rotate the four-patch units as shown. The border strips should measure 3½" x 27½". Sew the borders to the top and bottom of the center block. Press the seam allowances toward the center block.

7. Sew red 3½" x 27½" middle-border strips to the sides of the quilt top. Press the seam allowances toward the red border strips. Sew red 3½" x 33½" strips to the top and bottom of the quilt top. Press the seam allowances toward the red border strips.

8. Draw a diagonal line from corner to corner on the wrong side of the 16 assorted cream-print 2½" squares. Place marked squares on opposite corners of a green 4½" square, right sides together, with the drawn lines as shown. Sew on the drawn lines. Trim ¼" from the stitching lines. Press the seam allowances toward the cream triangles. Repeat on the remaining corners. Repeat to make a total of four square-in-a-square units.

Make 4.

9. Sew an assorted cream-print 3½" x 42" strip to an assorted green-print 1½" x 42" strip along the long edges to make a strip set. Press the seam allowances toward the green strip. Repeat to make a total of six strip sets. Crosscut the strip sets into 132 segments, 1½" wide.

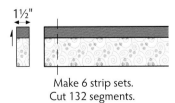

Make 6 strip sets.
Cut 132 segments.

10. Sew 33 segments from step 9 together along the long edges, turning every other segment 180° so the green squares are on alternating sides of the strip. Press the seam allowances in one direction. The border strip should measure 4½" x 33½". Repeat to make a total of four outer-border strips.

11. Sew outer-border strips to the left and right sides of the quilt top. Press the seam allowances toward the middle border. Sew a green square-in-a-square unit from step 8 to each end of the remaining two outer-border strips. Press the seam allowances toward the units. Sew these border strips to the top and bottom of the quilt top. Press the seam allowances toward the middle border.

Quilt assembly

FINISHING

1. Layer the quilt top with batting and backing. I used wool batting in this quilt, so you can really see the quilting.

2. Quilt as desired.

3. Bind the edges with the red-and-white print 2¼" x 42" strips.

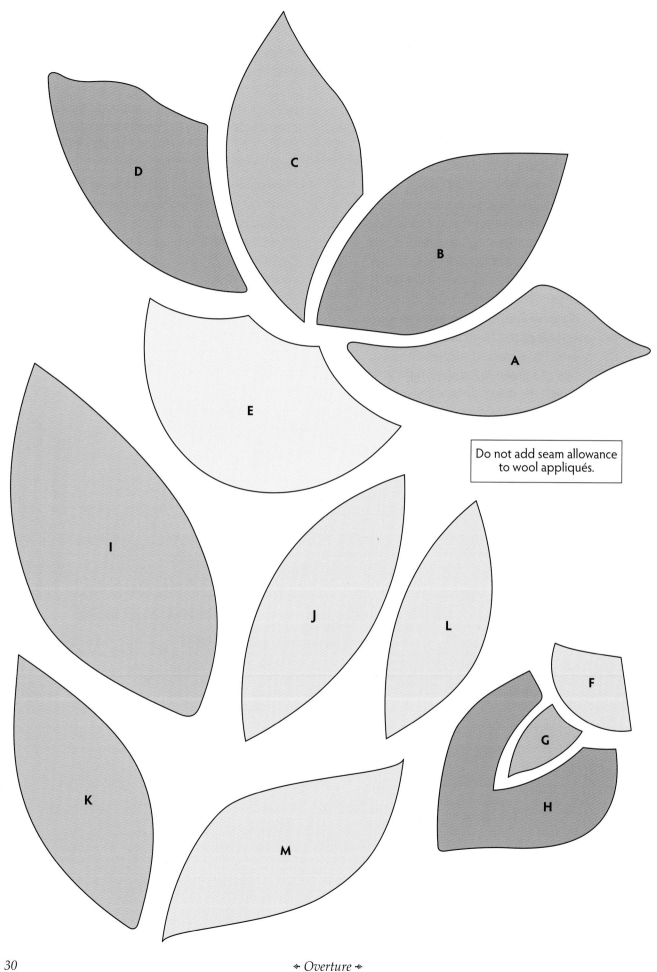

Do not add seam allowance to wool appliqués.

LET'S GET TOGETHER

The family room is where everyone gathers to relax, visit, and enjoy one another. Warm and cozy, quilts add so much both physically and visually to this space in your home. Curl up in one of these quilts or stack a group on a shelf or hearth just to look at!

POSY PARTY

Finished quilt size: 63½" x 75½" · Finished block size: 12" x 12"

Pieced and appliquéd by Margaret Brockbank; quilted by Maika Christensen

Graphic black and white are mixed with pops of color in this charming lap quilt. The piecing is simple—just 16 identical blocks embellished with a whole variety of blooms. You can add soft or bright colors—whatever works for you. This will be a favorite of everyone who gathers in your family room.

MATERIALS

Yardage is based on 42"-wide fabric.

3⅓ yards of cream print for blocks and middle border

1⅞ yards of black print for blocks, inner border, and binding

1 yard *total* of assorted green fabrics for appliquéd leaves and pieced outer border

½ yard of green fabric for stems

½ yard *total* of assorted red fabrics for flower appliqués and pieced outer border

½ yard *total* of assorted yellow fabrics for flower appliqués and pieced outer border

½ yard *total* of assorted orange fabrics for flower appliqués and pieced outer border

½ yard *total* of assorted pink fabrics for flower appliqués and pieced outer border

½ yard *total* of assorted blue fabrics for flower appliqués and pieced outer border

4 yards of fabric for backing

70" x 82" piece of batting

⅜" bias-tape maker

Freezer paper

Spray starch or sizing

Jillily Studio Appli-Glue (optional)

CUTTING

Refer to "Appliqué the Jillily Way" on page 10 and use patterns A and B on page 36 to make templates for cutting the appliqué pieces.

From the black print, cut:

3 strips, 4" x 42"; crosscut into 24 squares, 4" x 4"

5 strips, 3½" x 42"; crosscut into 48 squares, 3½" x 3½"

5 strips, 2" x 42"

8 strips, 2¼" x 42"

Continued on page 34.

From the cream print, cut:

4 strips, 9½" x 42"; crosscut into 16 squares, 9½" x 9½"

3 strips, 9½" x 42"

3 strips, 6½" x 42"; crosscut into 32 rectangles, 3½" x 6½"

3 strips, 4" x 42"; crosscut into 24 squares, 4" x 4"

3 strips, 3½" x 42"

From the *bias* of the green fabric for stems, cut:

Enough ⅞"-wide strips to equal a total of approximately 310"

From the assorted green fabrics, cut a *total* of:

96 of B

16 rectangles, 3½" wide and random lengths from 2½" to 7" long

From the assorted red, yellow, orange, pink, and blue fabrics, cut a *total* of:

8 strips, 3½" x 42"; crosscut into random lengths from 2½" to 7" long

66 of A

PIECING THE BLOCKS

1. Draw a diagonal line from corner to corner on the wrong side of each cream-print 4" square and each black-print 3½" square.

2. Place a marked cream-print square on top of a black-print 4" square, right sides together. Sew ¼" from both sides of the marked line. Cut the squares apart on the marked line to make two half-square-triangle units. Press the seam allowances toward the black triangles. Trim each unit to 3½" x 3½". Repeat to make a total of 48 half-square-triangle units.

Make 48.

3. Place a marked black-print 3½" square on one end of a cream-print 3½" x 6½" rectangle as shown, right sides together and raw edges aligned. Stitch on the marked line. Trim ¼" from the stitching line. Press the seam allowances

toward the black triangle. Repeat to make a total of 16 rectangle units.

Make 16.

4. Repeat step 3, positioning the marked line as shown, to make 16 additional rectangle units.

Make 16.

5. Place a marked black square on one corner of a cream 9½" square as shown, right sides together and raw edges aligned. Stitch on the drawn line. Trim ¼" from the stitching line. Press the seam allowances toward the black triangle. Repeat to make a total of 16 units.

Make 16.

6. Sew a half-square-triangle unit from step 2 to a rectangle unit from step 3 as shown. Press the seam allowances toward the rectangle unit. Repeat to make a total of 16 units.

Make 16.

7. Sew a unit from step 6 to the bottom of a unit from step 5. Press the seam allowances toward the unit from step 6. Repeat to make a total of 16 units.

Make 16.

8. Sew two half-square-triangle units to a rectangle unit from step 4 as shown. Press the seam allowances toward the rectangle. Repeat to make a total of 16 units.

Make 16.

9. Sew a unit from step 8 to a unit from step 7 as shown. Press the seam allowances toward the unit from step 7. Repeat to make a total of 16 blocks. The blocks should measure 12½" x 12½".

Make 16.

APPLIQUÉING THE BLOCKS AND MIDDLE BORDER

Refer to "Appliqué the Jillily Way" on page 10 to prepare, position, and stitch the appliqué pieces.

1. Prepare appliqué pieces A and B.

2. Use the ⅞"-wide bias strips and bias-tape maker to make bias tape. Cut the bias tape into 16 pieces, 3" long, for the center stems and 32 pieces, 8" long, for the side stems.

3. Refer to the block appliqué placement diagram to position the stems and then pieces A and B on each block, trimming the stems as needed. Set aside the remaining pieces for the middle border. Glue baste the pieces in place using Jillily Studio Appli-Glue.

Block appliqué placement

4. Join the three cream 9½" x 42" strips end to end to make one long strip. From the pieced strip, cut two 57½"-long strips for the middle top and bottom borders. Refer to the border placement diagram to position the remaining stems and A and B pieces on the border strips, trimming the stems as needed. Glue baste the pieces in place.

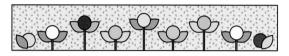

Middle top/bottom center border appliqué placement

5. Hand or machine stitch the appliqués in place.

ASSEMBLING THE QUILT TOP

1. Refer to the quilt assembly diagram on page 36 to lay out the appliquéd blocks in four rows of four blocks each. Sew the blocks in each row together. Press the seam allowances in opposite directions from row to row. Sew the rows together. Press the seam allowances in one direction. The quilt center should measure 48½" x 48½".

2. Join the five black-print 2" x 42" strips end to end to make one long strip. From the pieced strip, cut two 48½"-long strips and two 51½"-long strips for the inner border.

3. Sew the 48½"-long strips to the sides of the quilt center. Press the seam allowances toward the inner-border strips. Sew the 51½"-long strips to the top and bottom of the quilt center. Press the seam allowances toward the inner-border strips.

4. Join the three cream-print 3½" x 42" strips end to end to make one long strip. From the pieced strip, cut two 51½"-long strips for the middle side borders. Sew these strips to the sides of the quilt top. Press the seam allowances toward the inner border.

5. Sew the appliquéd middle top and bottom borders to the top and bottom of the quilt top, placing the base of the flowers against the inner border. Press the seam allowances toward the inner border.

6. Randomly sew the assorted green, red, yellow, orange, pink, and blue 3½"-wide pieces together to make one long strip. From the pieced strip, cut two 69½"-long strips and two 75½"-long strips for the outer border.

7. Sew the 69½"-long strips to the sides of the quilt top. Press the seam allowances toward the outer-border strips. Sew the 75½"-long strips to the top and bottom of the quilt top. Press the seam allowances toward the outer-border strips.

FINISHING

1. Layer the quilt top with batting and backing. I used 100% cotton batting in this quilt.

2. Quilt as desired.

3. Bind the edges with the black 2¼" x 42" strips.

Quilt assembly

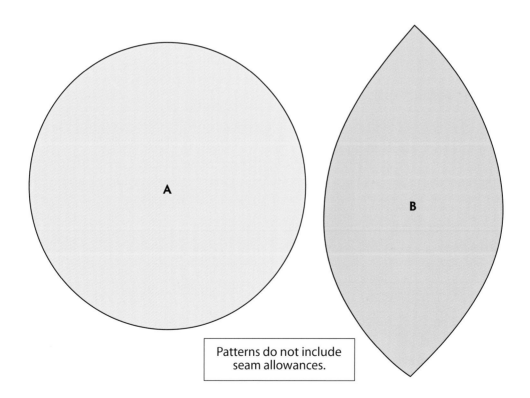

A

B

Patterns do not include seam allowances.

PATIO TILES

Finished runner size: 12" x 33"

By Jill Finley

What a fun runner to display in your family room! Plaid and checked felted wools keep the flowers from being too frilly. This project goes together quickly—there's no piecing, and the wool appliqués don't need their edges turned under. Finished off with a cotton back and binding, this is a runner that everyone will enjoy.

MATERIALS

Yardage is based on 42"-wide fabric.

12" x 38" piece of cream felted wool for runner background and flower appliqués

7" x 20" piece of dark-gray felted wool for flower-appliqué backgrounds

6" x 6" square of red felted wool for flower and tile appliqués

6" x 6" square of green felted wool for leaf and tile appliqués

12" x 12" square *total* of assorted gray felted wools for tiles

12" x 12" square *total* of assorted red felted wools for tiles

12" x 12" square *total* of assorted green felted wools for tiles

12" x 12" square *total* of assorted black felted wools for tiles

Small pieces of red and green wool roving for flower and leaf details

¼ yard of black cotton print for binding

⅓ yard of cotton fabric for backing

Felting needle

Small piece of craft foam

Jillily Studio Appli-Glue (optional)

2 skeins of #8 black pearl cotton

Size 5 embroidery needle

CUTTING

Refer to "Appliqué the Jillily Way" on page 10 and use patterns A–G on page 40 to make templates for cutting the appliqué pieces.

From the dark-gray felted wool, cut:

1 rectangle, 6½" x 9"

2 rectangles, 4½" x 6½"

From the cream felted wool, cut:

1 rectangle, 12" x 33"

1 of A

4 of F

Continued on page 39.

From the red felted wool for flower and tile appliqués, cut:
2 *each* of D and E
6 squares, 1½" x 1½"

From the green felted wool for leaf and tile appliqués, cut:
1 *each* of B and C
2 of G
6 squares, 1½" x 1½"

From the assorted gray, red, green, and black felted wools, cut a *total* of:
34 squares, 1½" x 1½"

From the fabric for backing, cut:
1 rectangle, 12" x 33"

From the black-cotton print, cut:
3 strips, 2¼" x 42"

APPLIQUÉING THE RUNNER TOP

1. Referring to "Working with Wool" on page 7, "Positioning the Appliqués" on page 13, and the appliqué placement diagrams below, arrange the appliqués on the dark-gray rectangles. Glue baste the pieces in place using Jillily Studio Appli-Glue.

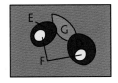

Side rectangle appliqué placement.
Make 1 and 1 reversed.

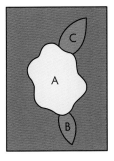

Center rectangle appliqué placement.
Make 1.

2. Using one strand of black pearl cotton and the embroidery needle, blanket-stitch around all of the pieces except for the F flower centers. Refer to the pattern to stitch three French knots in the center of each F piece.

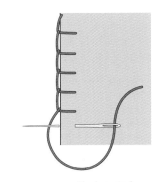

Blanket stitch

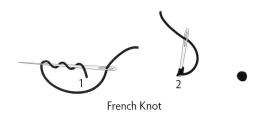

French Knot

3. Referring to the pattern and the photo on page 37, use the red roving pieces to create a swirl design in the center of the A flower. Place the wool rectangle on the foam scrap and use the felting needle to apply the roving by punching it repeatedly. The fibers of the roving and the fibers in the cream wool beneath it will merge and lock together. Keep the edges of your roving design crisp by twisting the roving as you apply it. Use the same method to apply the green roving detail to the leaves.

4. Pull a few threads from the edge of the leftover cream felted wool. Swirl them tightly to make a small dot about ¼" in diameter. Use your felting needle to punch these onto the background of the appliquéd side and center rectangles where shown on the pattern and in the photo.

5. Trim the side rectangles to 4" x 6" and the center rectangle to 6" x 8¾".

6. Center the appliquéd center rectangle on the cream 12" x 33" background rectangle. Center the appliquéd side rectangles between the center rectangle and the ends of the background rectangle. Arrange 15 assorted wool 1½" squares on point along the long sides of the background rectangle, placing them about ½" from the edge of the background. Add three assorted wool 1½" squares on point at each end and between the appliquéd rectangles. You'll have four squares left over.

7. Blanket-stitch around the 1½" squares and the appliquéd rectangles with black pearl cotton.

FINISHING

1. Place the completed wool top over the backing rectangle, wrong sides together. Pin in place around all of the edges. Use a walking foot to baste around the edges.

2. Bind the edges with the black 2¼" x 42" strips.

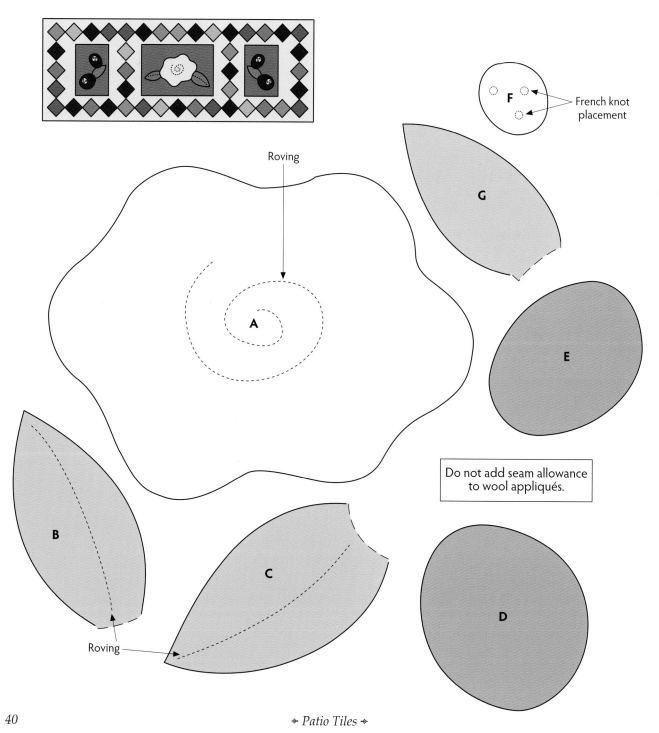

Roving

F — French knot placement

G

A

E

Do not add seam allowance to wool appliqués.

B

C

D

Roving

WINDING DOWN

Finished quilt size: 56½" x 74½" · Finished block size: 6" x 6"

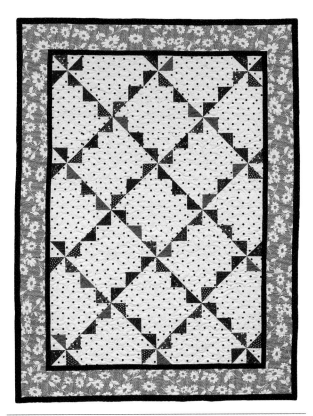

Pieced by Jill Finley; quilted by Maika Christensen

This sweet quilt is bold and cheery, relaxed and striking. It invites the feeling of fun to your home. It reminds me of leisurely hours spent playing board games, having long conversations, and watching ball games with friends and family. Put this quilt together in a weekend and be ready for your next get-together, where you can relax and wind down from your busy week.

MATERIALS

Yardage is based on 42"-wide fabric.

2½ yards of cream dotted print for blocks and sashing

1⅛ yards of black print for inner border, outer border, and binding

1⅛ yards of red floral for middle border

⅔ yard *total* of assorted red prints for blocks and sashing

3½ *yards* of fabric for backing

63" x 81" piece of batting

CUTTING

From the cream dotted print, cut:

5 strips, 4" x 42"; crosscut into 48 squares, 4" x 4"

9 strips, 6½" x 42"; crosscut into:

    11 rectangles, 6½" x 12½"

    6 rectangles, 6½" x 9½"

    30 rectangles, 3½" x 6½"

From the assorted red prints, cut a *total* of:

5 strips, 4" x 42"; crosscut into 48 squares, 4" x 4"

From the black print, cut:

13 strips, 1½" x 42"

7 strips, 2¼" x 42"

From the red floral, cut:

6 strips, 5½" x 42"

PIECING THE BLOCKS

1. Draw a diagonal line from corner to corner on the wrong side of each cream dotted-print 4" square. Place a marked square on top of a red-print 4" square, right sides together. Sew ¼" from both sides of the marked line. Cut the squares apart on the marked line to make two half-square-triangle units. Press the seam

allowances toward the red triangles. Trim the units to 3½" x 3½". Repeat to make a total of 96 half-square-triangle units.

Make 96.

2. Sew two half-square-triangle units together as shown, nesting the seam allowances so the points meet exactly. Repeat to make a total of 12 pairs. Press the seam allowances of each pair in the same direction.

Make 12.

3. Join two pairs from step 2 to make a clockwise-spinning Pinwheel block. Repeat to make a total of six blocks. To press, remove the stitching in the seam allowances at the center of the block, and press the seam allowances in opposite directions so they spiral around the center and lie flat. The blocks should measure 6½" x 6½".

Clockwise Pinwheel block.
Make 6.

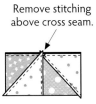

Remove stitching above cross seam.

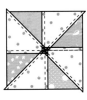

Back of block

4. Repeat steps 2 and 3 with four of the remaining half-square-triangle units, orienting the units so that the pinwheels rotate counterclockwise as shown. Repeat to make a total of 12

counterclockwise Pinwheel blocks. Press the seam allowances as described in step 3.

Counterclockwise Pinwheel block.
Make 12.

ASSEMBLING THE QUILT TOP

1. Alternately lay out three counterclockwise-spinning Pinwheel blocks along with two cream dotted print 6½" x 12½" rectangles. Sew the pieces together to make block row A. Press the seam allowances toward the rectangles. Repeat to make a total of four rows. The rows should measure 6½" x 42½".

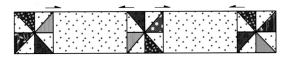

Block row A.
Make 4.

2. Lay out two clockwise-spinning Pinwheel blocks, one cream dotted-print 6½" x 12½" rectangle, and two cream dotted-print 6½" x 9½" rectangles as shown. Sew the pieces together to make block row B. Repeat to make a total of three rows. The rows should measure 6½" x 42½".

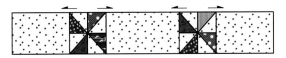

Block row B.
Make 3.

3. Lay out five cream dotted-print 3½" x 6½" rectangles and four half-square-triangle units as shown. Sew the pieces together to make a sashing row. Repeat to make a total of six rows. The rows should measure 3½" x 42½".

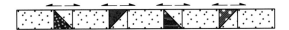

Sashing row.
Make 6.

4. Refer to the quilt assembly diagram below to lay out the block rows and sashing rows, rotating every other sashing row to create the pattern. Sew the rows together. Press the seam allowances toward the sashing rows.

5. Join the black-print 1½" x 42" strips end to end to make one long strip. From the pieced strip, cut two 60½"-long strips and two 44½"-long strips for the inner border. Set the remainder of the black strip aside. Sew the 60½"-long inner-border strips to the sides of the quilt center. Press the seam allowances toward the inner-border strips. Sew the 44½"-long inner-border strips to the top and bottom of the quilt center. Press the seam allowances toward the inner-border strips.

6. Join the red floral 5½" x 42" strips end to end to make one long strip. From the pieced strip, cut two 62½"-long strips and two 54½"-long strips for the middle border. Sew the 62½"-long strips to the sides of the quilt top. Press the seam allowances toward the inner border. Sew the 54½"-long strips to the top and bottom of the quilt top. Press the seam allowances toward the inner border.

7. From the remainder of the pieced black strip, cut two 72½"-long strips and two 56½"-long strips for the outer border. Sew the 72½"-long strips to the sides of the quilt top. Press the seam allowances toward the outer border. Sew the 56½"-long strips to the top and bottom of the quilt top. Press the seam allowances toward the outer border.

FINISHING

1. Layer the quilt top with batting and backing. I used wool batting in this quilt.

2. Quilt as desired.

3. Bind the edges with the black 2¼" x 42" strips.

Quilt assembly

HEART *of the* HOME

The kitchen is filled with hard surfaces, so it's the perfect place to add a quilt or two! I love to use a quilt as a decorative table topper. It adds so much more dimension, color, and pattern to that surface. Top your counter or island with a runner to add another decorative touch, and just for fun, embellish your dish towels with some piecing!

BERRY PATCH

Finished quilt size: 64½" x 64½"

*Pieced and appliquéd by Jill Finley;
quilted by Maika Christensen*

This yummy table topper will take your thoughts right to a roadside fruit stand every time you look at it. Sweet summer berries are advertised just like the signs I watch for at the stands near my home when the berries are finally ripe. The cheerful lettering is simple to do with prepared bias strips, and the appliqué pieces are large and quick to stitch.

MATERIALS

Yardage is based on 42"-wide fabric.

2⅛ yards of black print for blocks, letters, scalloped border, blackberry appliqués, and binding

2 yards of white print #2 for quilt-border background

1¼ yards of green print for blocks, inner and outer borders, and leaf appliqués

¾ yard of white print #1 for quilt-center background

½ yard *total* of assorted red prints for blocks and strawberry and raspberry appliqués

½ yard *total* of assorted blue prints for blocks and blueberry and blackberry appliqués

⅜ yard *total* of assorted black prints for blocks and blackberry appliqués

3⅞ yards of fabric for backing

68" x 68" square of batting

⅜" bias-tape maker

Freezer paper

Spray starch or sizing

Jillily Studio Appli-Glue (optional)

Scallop ruler (optional, see page 53)

CUTTING

Refer to "Appliqué the Jillily Way" on page 10 and use patterns A–BB on pages 54–58 to make templates for cutting the appliqué pieces. For pieces A, C, E, W, Y, and AA, use the marked line to make a template, but be sure to add at least ¼" for a seam allowance. Use the same marked line as a turn-under guide for reverse appliqué on pieces B, D, F, X, Z, and BB.

From white print #1, cut:

3 strips, 4½" x 42"; crosscut into 6 strips, 4½" x 21"

4 strips, 2½" x 42"; crosscut into 24 rectangles, 2½" x 6½"

From the assorted red prints, cut a *total* of:

3 strips, 2½" x 42"; crosscut into:

    4 strips, 2½" x 21"

    9 squares, 2½" x 2½"

1 *each* of P, Q, U, V, W, X, Y, Z, AA, and BB

Continued on page 48.

From the assorted blue prints, cut a *total* of:

2 strips, 2½" x 42"; crosscut into 3 strips, 2½" x 21"

1 *each* of G, H, I, J, K, L, M, N, and O

From the black print, cut:

1 rectangle, 24" x 42"; cut into enough ⅞"-wide *bias* strips to equal approximately 825"

14 strips, 2" x 42"

7 strips, 2½" x 42"

From the remainder of the black print and the assorted black prints, cut a *total* of:

3 strips, 2½" x 21"

8 squares, 2½" x 2½"

1 *each* of A, B, C, D, E, and F

From white print #2, cut:

4 strips, 11½" x 38½" (These strips are for the appliquéd borders. You may want to cut them a little larger and trim them down to size after you're done appliquéing.)

2 strips, 4½" x 42"; crosscut into 4 strips, 4½" x 21"

2 strips, 2½" x 42"; crosscut into:

    4 rectangles, 2½" x 6½"

    4 rectangles, 2½" x 3½"

    4 squares, 2½" x 2½"

2 strips, 1½" x 42"; crosscut into:

    4 rectangles, 1½" x 11½"

    4 rectangles, 1½" x 6½"

From the green print, cut:

4 strips, 4½" x 42"; crosscut into:

    4 rectangles, 4½" x 16½"

    4 rectangles, 4½" x 12½"

    16 squares, 2½" x 2½"

7 strips, 2½" x 42"

2 *each* of R, S, and T

PIECING THE QUILT CENTER

1. Sew 4½" x 21" white print #1 strips to two red, two black, and two 2½" x 21" blue strips along the long edges to make six strip sets. Press the seam allowances toward the red, black, and blue

strips. Crosscut each pair of strip sets from the same color family into 16 segments, 2½" wide.

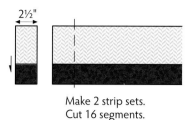

Make 2 strip sets.
Cut 16 segments.

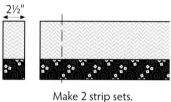

Make 2 strip sets.
Cut 16 segments.

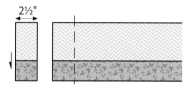

Make 2 strip sets.
Cut 16 segments.

2. Lay out one red, one blue, and one black segment as shown to make block A. Sew the segments for the block together. Press the seam allowances toward the blue and black segments. Repeat to make a total of eight blocks. The blocks should measure 6½" x 6½".

Block A.
Make 8.

3. Repeat step 2 with the remaining segments, arranging the segments as shown to make eight of block B.

Block B.
Make 8.

4. Lay out two A blocks and two B blocks with three 2½" x 6½" white print #1 rectangles as shown to make rows 1–4, paying careful attention to how the blocks are rotated in each row. Sew the pieces in each row together. Press the seam allowances toward the blocks. The rows should measure 6½" x 30½".

Row 1.
Make 1.

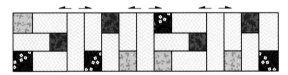

Row 2.
Make 1.

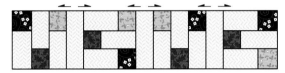

Row 3.
Make 1.

Row 4.
Make 1.

5. Lay out four 2½" x 6½" white print #1 rectangles, two 2½" green squares, and one 2½" red square as shown. Sew the pieces together to make sashing row A. Press the seam allowances toward the squares. Repeat to make a total of two rows. The rows should measure 2½" x 30½".

Sashing row A.
Make 2.

6. Alternately lay out four 2½" x 6½" white print #1 rectangles and three 2½" red squares. Sew the

pieces together to make sashing row B. Press the seam allowances toward the squares. The row should measure 2½" x 30½".

Sashing row B.
Make 1.

7. Sew a sashing row A between block rows 1 and 2. Sew the remaining sashing row A between block rows 3 and 4. Sew sashing row B between block rows 2 and 3 to join the quilt center. Press the seam allowances toward the sashing rows. The quilt center should measure 30½" x 30½".

PIECING AND ADDING THE INNER BORDER

1. Sew a 2½" red square between two 2½" green squares. Press the seam allowances toward the red square. Repeat to make a total of four units. Sew a 2½" green square between two 2½" black squares. Press the seam allowances toward the black squares. Repeat to make a total of four units. Sew a green-red-green unit to a black-green-black unit as shown. Repeat to make a total of four border-center units. The units should measure 4½" x 6½".

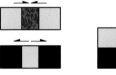

Make 4.

2. Sew a 4½" x 12½" green rectangle to each short side of a center unit from step 1 as shown. Press the seam allowances toward the green rectangles. Repeat to make a total of two borders. The borders should measure 4½" x 30½". Refer to the quilt assembly diagram on page 53 to sew these borders to the sides of the quilt center, with the red squares next to the quilt center.

Side border.
Make 2.

3. Refer to the quilt assembly diagram to sew a 4½" x 16½" green rectangle to each short side of a center unit from step 1 as shown. Press the seam allowances toward the green rectangles. Repeat to make a total of two borders. The borders should measure 4½" x 38½". Sew these borders to the top and bottom of the quilt center, with the red squares next to the quilt center. The quilt top should now measure 38½" x 38½".

MAKING AND ADDING THE MIDDLE BORDER

1. Lightly press the 11½" x 38½" white print #2 middle-border strips in half lengthwise and crosswise to mark the centers. Fold the ends in to meet at the center and lightly press to divide the border into quarters. These will be your guide marks as you follow the placement diagram to arrange your appliqué pieces.

2. Referring to "Preparing Bias Tape" on page 12, use the ⅞"-wide black bias strips to make bias tape. Use the letter guides on pages 59–63 and shape the bias tape with a hot iron to make the letters needed to spell out the berry names.

3. Follow the placement diagrams on page 51 to lay out the letters on each border. Use Jillily Studio Appli-Glue to glue baste the letters in place, turning under the raw edges on the ends of each one. Using black thread, machine top-stitch each letter in place.

4. Refer to "Appliqué the Jillily Way" to prepare appliqué pieces A–BB. Place the prepared appliqué pieces onto each border, following the placement guides and placing the "inside" of the blackberry and raspberry shapes (pieces A, C, E, W, Y, and AA) under the openings for the appropriate shapes. Glue baste the pieces in place. Using matching thread and an appliqué stitch, hand stitch each appliqué in place. If you cut your border strips larger than needed, trim them to 11½" x 38½".

5. Sew 4½" x 21" white print #2 strips to two red, one black, and one blue 2½" x 21" strip along the long edges to make four strip sets. Press the seam allowances toward the red, black, and blue strips. Crosscut the red strip sets into 12 segments, 2½" wide, and the black and blue strip sets each into eight segments, 2½" wide.

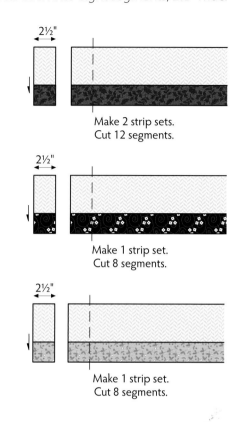

2½"

Make 2 strip sets.
Cut 12 segments.

2½"

Make 1 strip set.
Cut 8 segments.

2½"

Make 1 strip set.
Cut 8 segments.

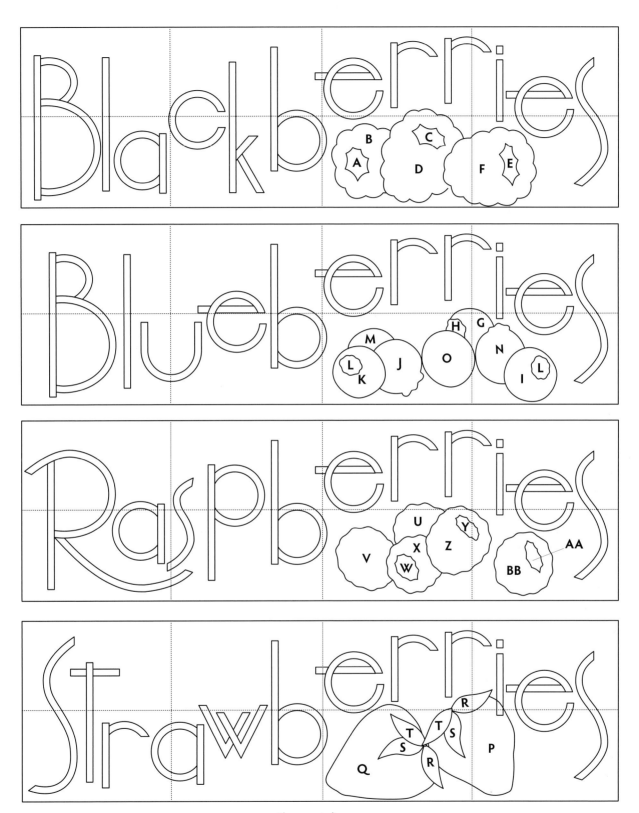

Placement diagrams

6. Lay out one red, one blue, and one black segment from step 5 as shown. Sew the segments together. Press the seam allowances toward the red and black segments. Repeat to make a total of four units. The units should measure 6½" x 6½".

Make 4.

7. Sew a 2½" x 6½" white print #2 rectangle to the long edge of four of the remaining red segments from step 5. Press the seam allowances toward the red segment. Sew each of these units to a unit from step 6 as shown. Press the seam allowances toward the unit from step 6. Add a 1½" x 6½" white print #2 rectangle to the opposite side of each unit from step 6 as shown. Press the seam allowances toward the unit from step 6.

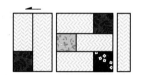 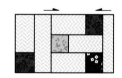

Make 4.

8. Sew a 2½" white print #2 square and a 2½" x 3½" white print #2 rectangle to each of the four remaining red segments from step 5. Press the seam allowances as shown.

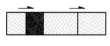

Make 4.

9. Sew a blue segment from step 5 to each of the four remaining black segments from step 5. Press the seam allowances toward the black segments. Trim 1" from the end of each black segment. The units should measure 2½" x 11½". Sew a 1½" x 11½" white print #2 rectangle to the top of each of these units. Press the seam allowances toward the segments from step 5.

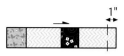

Make 4.

10. Sew each unit from step 9 to the top of a unit from step 8. Press the seam allowances toward the unit from step 8.

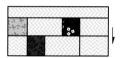

Make 4.

11. Sew a unit from step 10 to the top of each unit from step 7 to complete the corner blocks. The blocks should measure 11½" x 11½".

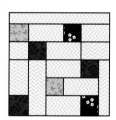

Make 4.

12. Refer to the quilt assembly diagram on page 53 to sew the strawberry and raspberry appliquéd borders to the sides of the quilt top. Press the seam allowances toward the inner border. Sew a corner block to each end of the blueberry and blackberry appliquéd borders. Press the seam allowances toward the blocks. Sew these borders to the top and bottom of the quilt top. Press the seam allowances toward the inner border.

ADDING THE OUTER BORDER

1. Sew three 2½" x 42" green-print strips together end to end to make one long strip. From the pieced strip, cut two 60½"-long strips. Sew these strips to the sides of the quilt top. Press the seam allowances toward the outer border.

2. Sew the remaining four 2½" x 42" green strips together end to end to make one long strip. From the pieced strip, cut two 64½"-long strips. Sew these strips to the top and bottom of the quilt top. Press the seam allowances toward the outer border.

FINISHING

1. Layer the quilt sandwich with batting and backing. I used wool batting on this quilt because it drapes so beautifully and really pops up to show the quilting details.

2. Quilt as desired. Use black thread to stitch "seeds" on the strawberry motifs, if desired.

3. To create the scalloped edging, refer to "Appliqué the Jillily Way" and use the scallop pattern on page 58 to make a freezer-paper template, or use the scallop ruler described at right. Trace the scallop design along the length of seven 2" x 42" black strips. Lay each strip right sides together with one of the remaining 2" x 42" black strips. Stitch on the drawn lines, leaving the long straight edge open. Trim around the scallops leaving a scant ¼" seam allowance. Turn each strip to the right side and press.

4. With the raw edges aligned, lay the black scalloped strips along the outer border. When you come to the end of one strip, lay another one next to it. There's no need to join the strips because the edges are finished. Adjust the strips so they're centered the same on each side. Baste the strips in place along the raw edges.

5. Bind the edges with the black 2½" x 42" strips.

Quilt assembly

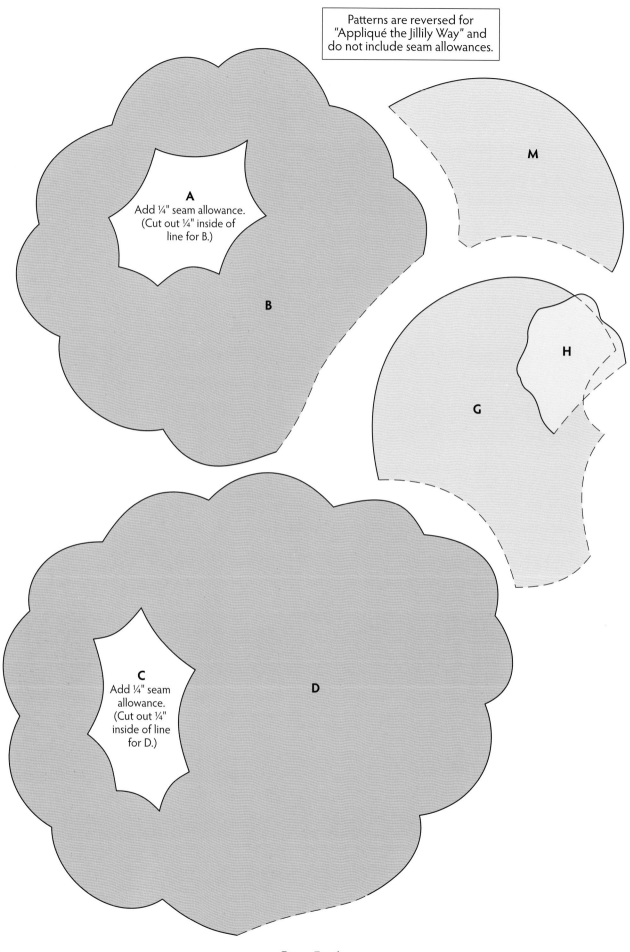

Patterns are reversed for "Appliqué the Jillily Way" and do not include seam allowances.

A
Add ¼" seam allowance.
(Cut out ¼" inside of line for B.)

B

M

H

G

C
Add ¼" seam allowance.
(Cut out ¼" inside of line for D.)

D

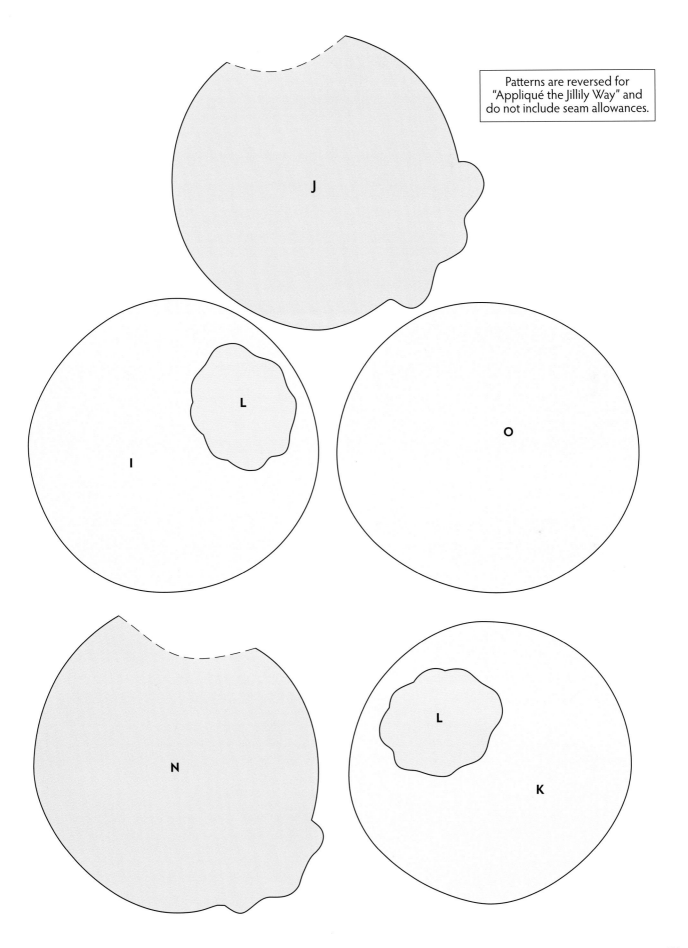

Patterns are reversed for
"Appliqué the Jillily Way" and
do not include seam allowances.

J

L

I

O

N

L

K

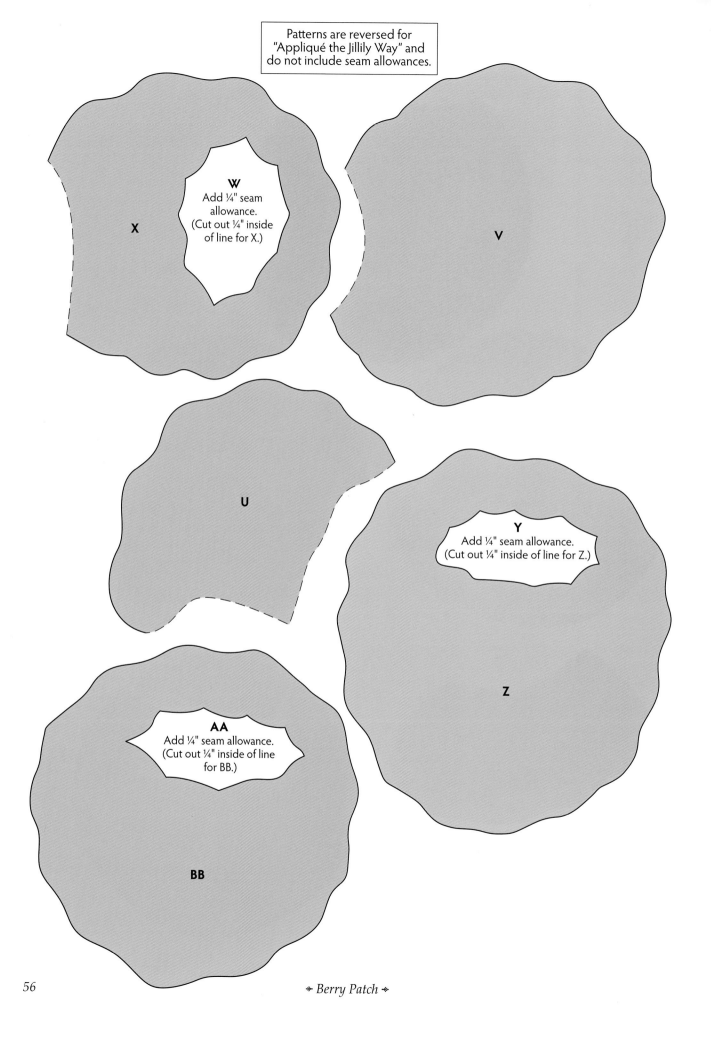

Patterns are reversed for
"Appliqué the Jillily Way" and
do not include seam allowances.

W
Add ¼" seam
allowance.
(Cut out ¼" inside
of line for X.)

X

V

U

Y
Add ¼" seam allowance.
(Cut out ¼" inside of line for Z.)

Z

AA
Add ¼" seam allowance.
(Cut out ¼" inside of line
for BB.)

BB

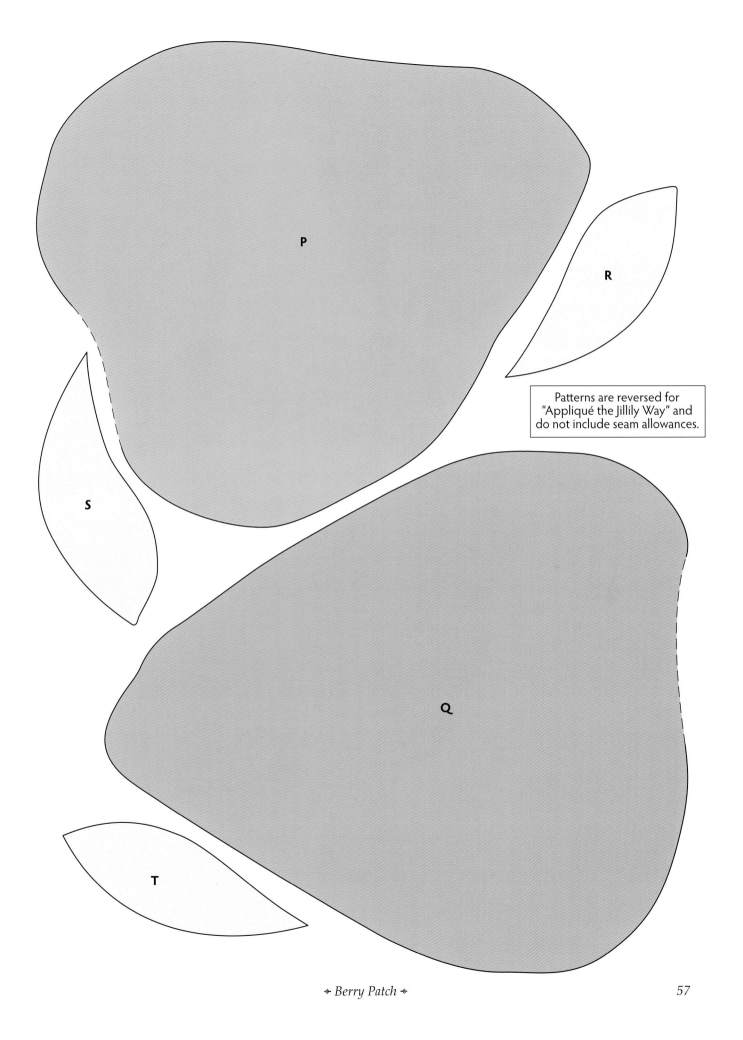

P

R

Patterns are reversed for "Appliqué the Jillily Way" and do not include seam allowances.

S

Q

T

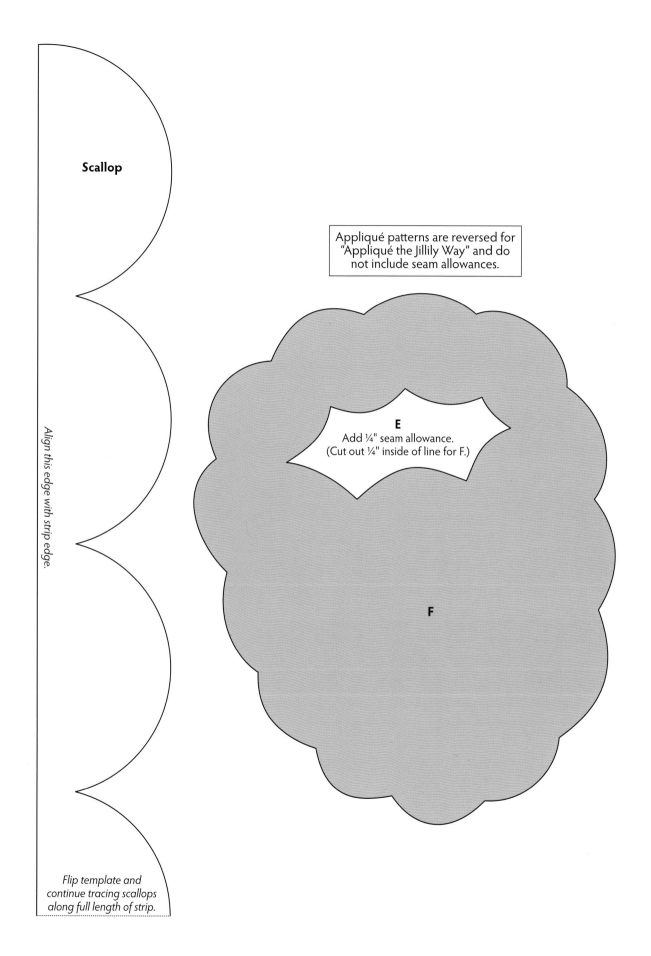

Scallop

Align this edge with strip edge.

Appliqué patterns are reversed for "Appliqué the Jillily Way" and do not include seam allowances.

E
Add ¼" seam allowance.
(Cut out ¼" inside of line for F.)

F

Flip template and continue tracing scallops along full length of strip.

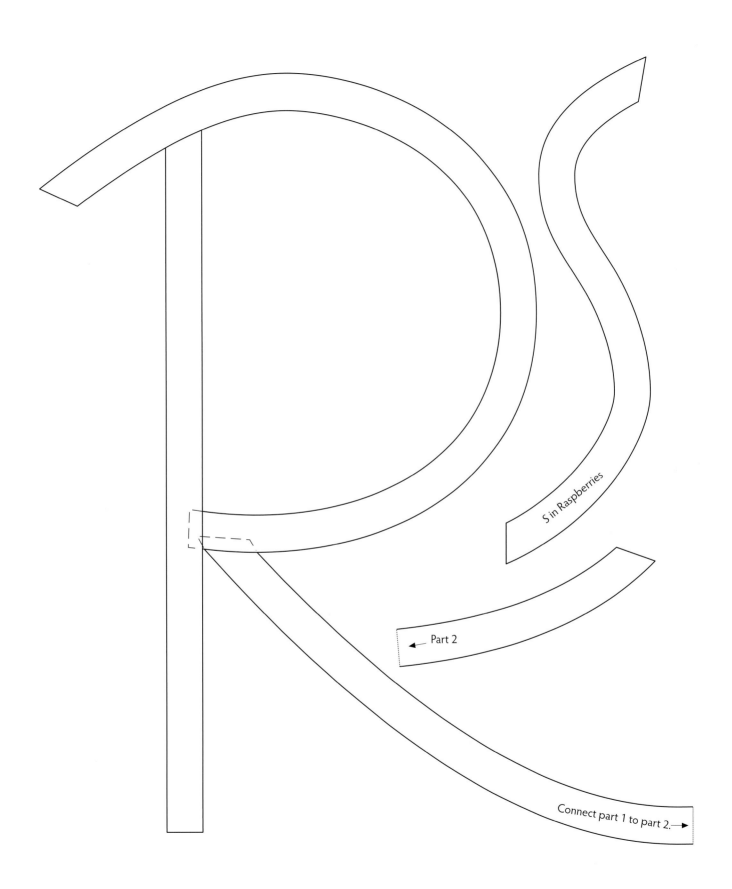

S in Raspberries

← Part 2

Connect part 1 to part 2.→

S in ... berries

⬥ *Berry Patch* ⬥

S in Straw ...

❖ *Berry Patch* ❖

CHERRY LEMONADE

Finished towel size: 28" x 29"

By Jill Finley

A little piecing, a little appliqué, and a bit of embroidery create cherries and lemons that dance their way across purchased flour-sack towels. Whip up some pretty dish towels for your kitchen or to give as a gift to your favorite cook.

MATERIALS

Yardage is based on 42"-wide fabric. Materials are enough to make one lemon and one cherry towel.

2 white flour-sack dish towels*

⅜ yard *total* of assorted light- and medium-green prints for pieced strips

¼ yard *total* of assorted red prints for pieced strips

¼ yard *total* of assorted yellow prints for pieced strips

¼ yard of dark-green fabric for leaf appliqués

Medium-green and dark-green embroidery floss

Size 7 embroidery needle

Freezer paper

Spray starch or sizing

Jillily Studio Appli-Glue (optional)

Dish towels are available at many craft and sewing stores. Prewash and dry towels before making the projects.

CUTTING

Refer to "Appliqué the Jillily Way" on page 10 and use patterns A and B on page 67 to make templates for cutting the appliqué pieces.

From the assorted light- and medium-green prints, cut a *total* of:

2 strips, 2½" x 28½"

18 squares, 2½" x 2½"

6 squares, 2¼" x 2¼"

2 rectangles, 2" x 6"

4 sets of 4 matching squares, 1⅛" x 1⅛" (16 total)

From the assorted yellow prints, cut a *total* of:

3 squares, 4½" x 4½"

18 squares, 2½" x 2½"

4 sets of 4 matching squares, 1⅛" x 1⅛" (16 total)

From the assorted red prints, cut a *total* of:

2 strips, 2½" x 28½"

8 squares, 2½" x 2½"

From the dark-green fabric, cut:

4 of A

3 of B

MAKING THE CHERRY TOWEL

1. Draw a diagonal line from corner to corner on the wrong side of each green and yellow 1⅛" square.

2. Select four matching green squares from step 1. Place a marked square on one corner of a red 2½" square, right sides together. Sew on the drawn line. Trim ¼" from the stitching line. Press the seam allowances toward the red square. Repeat on the remaining corners of the square to make a cherry unit. Repeat with the remaining red 2½" squares and green and yellow 1⅛" squares to make four cherry units with green corners and four cherry units with yellow corners.

Make 4 of each.

3. Arrange the cherry units and the green and yellow 2½" squares in two horizontal rows as shown. Sew the pieces in each row into pairs first, and then sew the pairs together to make each strip. Press the seam allowances in each row in opposite directions. Sew the strips together. Press the seam allowances in one direction. The strip should measure 4½" x 28½".

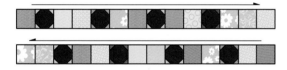

4. Sew a green 2½" x 28½" strip to each long edge of the cherry strip. Press the seam allowances toward the strips.

5. Use a pencil to lightly draw the stem lines for each pair of cherries onto the pieced strip.

Using three strands of dark-green floss and the embroidery needle, stem-stitch along the lines.

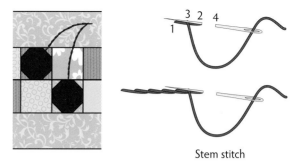

Stem stitch

6. Press under ¼" along each side of the cherry strip. Place the strip along the bottom edge of the dish towel, aligning the side and bottom edges. Using matching thread, topstitch along all four sides of the strip to secure it in place.

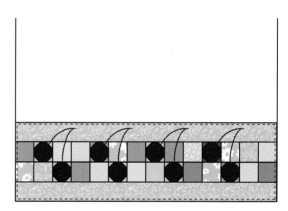

7. Refer to "Appliqué the Jillily Way" to prepare four A leaves. Place one leaf on each cherry stem as shown in the photo on page 65. The leaves will overlap onto the towel. Glue baste the leaves in place using Jillily Studio Appli-Glue. Using matching thread and an appliqué stitch, hand stitch each leaf in place.

8. Press under ½" along the long edges of a green 2" x 6" rectangle. Press the strip in half lengthwise, wrong sides together. Topstitch the folded-under edges together to make a hanging loop.

9. Place the hanging loop across an upper corner of the dish towel. Turn under the loop ends ½"

and topstitch across the ends with a boxed X as shown.

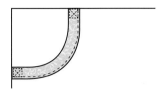

MAKING THE LEMON TOWEL

1. Draw a diagonal line from corner to corner on the wrong side of each green 2¼" square.

2. Place marked green squares on opposite corners of a yellow 4½" square, right sides together, with the drawn lines as shown. Sew on the drawn lines. Trim ¼" from the stitching lines. Press the seam allowances toward the yellow square. Repeat to make a total of three lemon units.

Make 3.

3. Arrange two yellow 2½" squares and two green 2½" squares in two horizontal rows as shown. Sew the squares in each row together. Press the seam allowances toward the green squares. Sew the rows together to make a four-patch unit. Repeat to make a total of four four-patch units.

4. Alternately lay out the four-patch units and lemon units into one row. Sew the units together. Press the seam allowances in one direction.

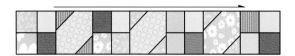

5. Sew a red 2½" x 28½" strip to each long edge of the lemon strip. Press the seam allowances toward the strips.

6. Use a pencil to lightly draw a stem at the top of each lemon unit as shown. Satin stitch the stem using three strands of medium-green embroidery floss. Take several single stitches at the stem base.

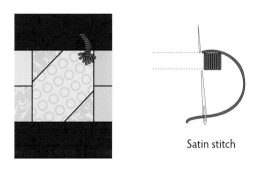

Satin stitch

7. Complete the towel as described in steps 6–9 of "Making the Cherry Towel," except use three B appliqués.

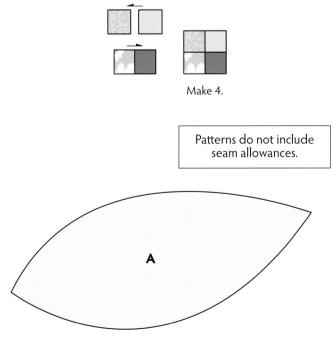

Make 4.

Patterns do not include seam allowances.

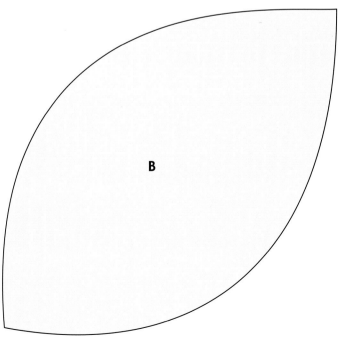

A

B

COTTAGE BLOOM

Finished runner size: 20½" x 36½"

*Pieced and appliquéd by Jill Finley;
quilted by Maika Christensen*

The secret to a well-dressed kitchen is in the details. This charming little runner will be the star of the show whether you lay it on your table, island, or counter. Vibrant colors paired with black always make a statement and give warmth to the space. Stitch up this yummy accessory to your culinary creations!

MATERIALS

Yardage is based on 42"-wide fabric.

½ yard of black print #1 for center background and middle pieced border

⅜ yard of green striped print for vines and pieced middle border

⅜ yard of red print for outer border

¼ yard *total* of assorted red prints for flower and berry appliqués and pieced middle border

¼ yard *total* of assorted green prints for leaf appliqués and pieced middle border

⅛ yard *total* of assorted yellow prints for flower appliqués and pieced middle border

⅛ yard of yellow print for inner border and pieced middle border

¼ yard of black print #2 for binding

⅔ yard of fabric for backing

24" x 40" piece of batting

¼" bias-tape maker

Freezer paper

Spray starch or sizing

Jillily Studio Appli-Glue (optional)

CUTTING

Refer to "Appliqué the Jillily Way" on page 10 and use patterns A–H on page 72 to make templates for cutting the appliqué pieces.

From the green striped print, cut:
Enough ⅝"-wide *bias* strips to equal approximately 44"
2 squares, 3" x 3"

From black print #1, cut:
1 rectangle, 9" x 25"
2 strips, 3" x 42"; crosscut into 20 squares, 3" x 3"

From the yellow print for inner border, cut:
2 strips, 1½" x 42"; crosscut into:
    2 strips, 1½" x 24½"
    2 strips, 1½" x 10½"

Continued on page 70.

From the remainder of the yellow print for border and the assorted yellow prints, cut a *total* of:

6 squares, 3" x 3"

1 of A

2 of E

From the assorted red prints, cut a *total* of:

7 squares, 3" x 3"

1 *each* of B, C, and D

6 of H

From the assorted green prints, cut a *total* of:

5 squares, 3" x 3"

3 of F

2 of G

From red print for outer border, cut:

3 strips, 3½" x 42"; crosscut into:

    2 strips, 3½" x 30½"

    2 strips, 3½" x 20½"

From black print #2, cut:

4 strips, 2¼" x 42"

APPLIQUÉING THE CENTER

Refer to "Appliqué the Jillily Way" to prepare, position, and stitch the appliqué pieces.

1. Prepare appliqué pieces A–H.

2. Use the ¼" bias-tape maker and the green striped ⅝"-wide bias strips to make bias tape.

3. Refer to the placement diagram to position the bias-tape stems and pieces A–H on the black print #1 rectangle. Glue baste the pieces in place using Jillily Studio Appli-Glue.

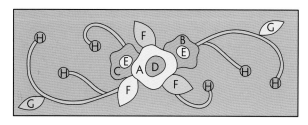

Appliqué placement

4. Hand or machine stitch the appliqués in place.

5. Press the runner center, and then trim to 8½" x 24½", keeping the design centered.

ADDING THE BORDERS

1. Sew a yellow-print 1½" x 24½" inner-border strip to each long side of the runner center. Press the seam allowances toward the inner border. Sew the yellow-print 1½" x 10½" inner-border strips to the short sides of the runner center. Press the seam allowances toward the inner border.

2. Draw a diagonal line from corner to corner on the wrong side of each black-print 3" square. Place a marked square on top of an assorted red-print 3" square, right sides together. Sew ¼" from both sides of the marked line. Cut the squares apart on the marked lines to make two half-square-triangle units. Press the seam allowances toward the black triangles. Trim each unit to 2½" x 2½". Repeat with the remaining assorted red, yellow, green, and green striped 3" squares to make a total of 40 half-square-triangle units.

Make 14.

Make 12.   Make 10.   Make 4.

3. Refer to the quilt assembly diagram on page 71 and randomly sew together 13 half-square-triangle units to make a row. Press the seam allowances toward the black triangles. Repeat to make a total of two rows. Sew these rows to the long sides of the runner top, with the black triangles against the inner border. Press the seam allowances toward the inner border.

4. Randomly sew together seven half-square-triangle units end to end to make a row, rotating the unit at one end of the strip as shown in the assembly diagram. Press the seam allowances toward the black triangles. Repeat to make a total of two rows. Sew these rows to the short sides of the runner top, with the black triangles against the inner border. Press the seam allowances toward the inner border.

5. Sew red-print 3½" x 30½" outer-border strips to the long sides of the runner top. Press the seam allowances toward the outer border. Sew red-print 3½" x 20½" outer-border strips to the short sides of the runner top. Press the seam allowances toward the outer border.

FINISHING

1. Layer the runner with batting and backing. I used 100% cotton batting in this quilt.
2. Quilt as desired.
3. Bind the edges with the black print #2 strips.

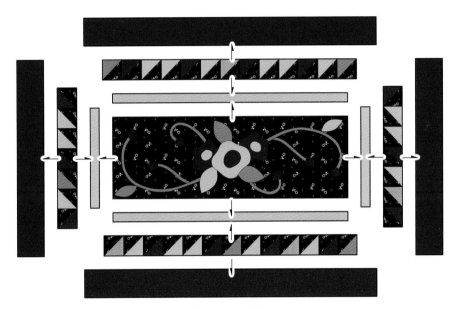

Quilt assembly

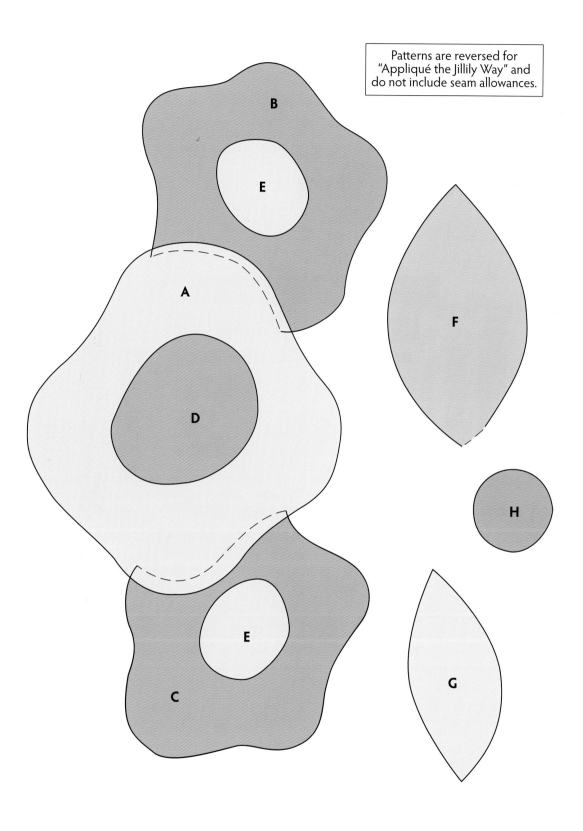

Patterns are reversed for
"Appliqué the Jillily Way" and
do not include seam allowances.

RESTFUL RETREAT

Naturally, a quilter's home would include quilts in the bedrooms. This collection is fresh and new with graceful lines and colors, creating unique rooms for your family and guests to enjoy. These beautiful quilts will make any bedroom a special retreat.

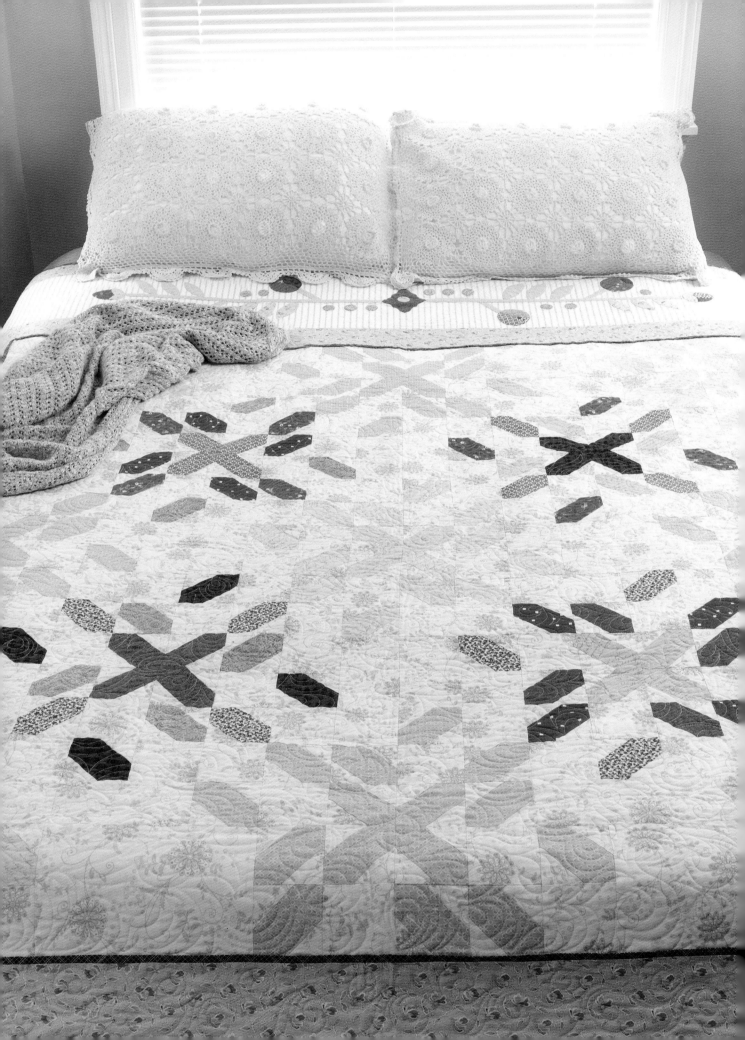

SHADOW BLOSSOM

Finished quilt size: 90½" x 90½" • Finished block size: 24" x 24"

*Pieced by Jill Finley; appliquéd by Jill Finley and
Margaret Brockbank; quilted by Tori Spencer*

Just a suggestion of large open blossoms and
their shadows are scattered across this quilt top.
The color scheme is inviting and restful with
the warm pinks, corals, and reds against the
cool, soothing blues and grays. This quilt adds
a touch of elegance and contemporary style to
your bedroom.

MATERIALS

Yardage is based on 42"-wide fabric.

3⅝ yards of white-and-gray print for quilt-center
   background

2⅓ yards of white-with-gray striped print for
   middle border

1⅞ yards of blue print for inner and outer borders
   and appliqués

1½ yards *total* of assorted red, coral, and pink prints
   for blocks and appliqués

1⅓ yards of light-blue print #1 for blocks and
   appliqués

1⅛ yards of red print for piping, appliqués, and
   binding

1 yard of light-blue print #2 for blocks and appliqués
   (This print should be slightly lighter than light-
   blue print #1.)

8 yards of fabric for backing

98" x 98" square of batting

½" bias-tape maker

Freezer paper

Spray starch or sizing

Jillily Studio Appli-Glue (optional)

CUTTING

*Refer to "Appliqué the Jillily Way" on page 10 and use
patterns A–L on page 82 to make templates for cutting
the appliqué pieces.*

From the white-and-gray print, cut:

14 strips, 3½" x 42"; crosscut into:
   8 rectangles, 3½" x 9½"
   24 rectangles, 3½" x 6½"
   84 squares, 3½" x 3½"

2 strips, 6½" x 42"; crosscut into 8 rectangles,
   6½" x 9½"

25 strips, 2¼" x 42"; crosscut into 408 squares,
   2¼" x 2¼"

Continued on page 76.

From the assorted red, coral, and pink prints, cut a *total* of:

16 sets of 4 matching squares, 3½" x 3½" (64 total)
8 *each* of A and B
16 *each* of E, F, G, and H
48 of L

From light-blue print #1, cut:

6 strips, 3½" x 42"; crosscut into 60 squares,
   3½" x 3½"
1 strip, 18" x 42"; cut into enough 1⅛"-wide bias
   strips to equal approximately 230"
8 of C
12 *each* of I and J

From light-blue print #2, cut:

8 strips, 3½" x 42"; crosscut into 72 squares,
   3½" x 3½"
8 of D

From the red print for piping, appliqués, and binding, cut:

10 strips, 2¼" x 42"
7 strips, 1" x 42"
4 of K

From the blue print for inner and outer borders, cut:

16 strips, 3½" x 42"
12 *each* of I and J

From the white-with-gray striped fabric, cut:

8 strips, 9½" x 42"

MAKING THE BLOCKS

1. Draw a diagonal line from corner to corner on the wrong side of each 2¼" white-and-gray print square. Place a marked square on top of a 3½" assorted red, coral, or pink square, right sides together. Sew on the drawn line. Trim ¼" from the stitching line. Press the seam allowances toward the red, coral, or pink. Repeat on the opposite corner. Press the seam allowances toward the white-and-gray print.

2. Repeat step 1 using all of the 3½" red, coral, and pink print squares *and* all of the 3½" light-blue print #1 and light-blue print #2 squares to make a total of 204 petal units. Keep the petals together by print to make assembly easier.

3. Select four different sets of four red, coral, and pink petal units. The instructions will refer to these units as red #1, red #2, red #3, and red #4.

4. Lay the four red #1 petal units in two horizontal rows of two units each as shown. Join the pieces in each row. Press the seam allowances in opposite directions. Sew the rows together to make the block center unit. Press the seam allowances in one direction.

Make 1.

5. Lay out a red #2 petal unit, a red #4 petal unit, and two 3½" white-and-gray squares into two horizontal rows as shown. Sew the pieces in each row together. Press the seam allowances toward the white-and-gray squares. Sew the rows together. Press the seam allowances in one direction. Add a 3½" x 6½" white-and-gray rectangle to the left side of this unit. Press the seam allowances toward the rectangle. Repeat to make a total of two units.

Make 2.

6. Sew the units from step 5 to the sides of the block center unit from step 4 to make the block center row. Press the seam allowances away from the center unit. The row should measure 6½" x 24½".

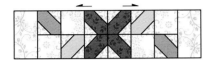

7. Lay out three light-blue print #2 petals and one 3½" white-and-gray print square in two horizontal rows as shown. Sew the pieces in each row together. Press the seam allowances in opposite directions. Sew the rows together. Press the seam allowances in one direction. Add a 3½" x 6½" white-and-gray rectangle to the bottom of the unit. Press the seam allowances toward the rectangle. Repeat to make a total of two light-blue units.

Make 2.

8. Lay out four light-blue print #1 petal units and two 3½" white-and-gray squares in three horizontal rows as shown. Sew the pieces in each row together. Press the seam allowances in opposite directions from row to row. Sew the rows together. Press the seam allowances in one direction. Repeat to make a total of two light-blue #1 units.

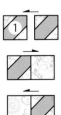

Make 2.

9. Sew a red #3 petal unit to a red #2 petal unit as shown. Press the seam allowances in one direction. Add a 3½" x 6½" white-and-gray rectangle to the top of the unit. Press the seam allowances toward the rectangle. Repeat to make a total of two units.

Make 2.

10. Lay out two 3½" white-and-gray squares, one red #4 petal unit, and one red #3 petal unit in two horizontal rows as shown. Sew the pieces in each row together. Press the seam allowances toward the white-and-gray squares. Sew the rows together. Press the seam allowances in one direction. Repeat to make a total of two units.

Make 2.

11. Lay out one unit from step 9, one unit from step 10, a light-blue print #2 petal unit, and a 3½" x 9½" white-and-gray rectangle in two horizontal rows. Sew the pieces in each row together. Press the seam allowances toward the rectangle and unit from step 9. Sew the rows together. Press the seam allowances in one direction. Repeat to make a total of two units.

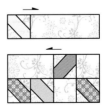 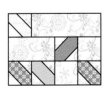

Make 2.

12. Sew a unit from step 7 to the left side of a unit from step 11. Sew a unit from step 8 to the right side of this unit. Press the seam allowances toward the unit from step 11. Repeat to make a total of two top rows. The rows should measure 9½" x 24½".

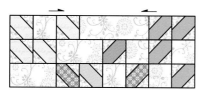

Make 2.

13. Sew the rows from step 12 to the top and bottom of the center row to complete the block. Press the seam allowances toward the top and bottom rows. The block should measure 24½" x 24½".

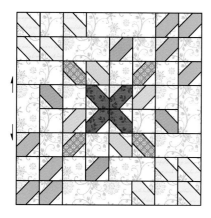

14. Repeat steps 3–13 to make a total of four blocks, varying the placement of the red prints so each block is different. Set aside the remaining petal units for the first border.

ASSEMBLING THE QUILT CENTER

1. Lay out the blocks in two rows of two blocks each, rotating the blocks to create the pattern. Sew the blocks in each row together. Press the seam allowances in opposite directions. Sew the rows together. The quilt center should measure 48½" x 48½".

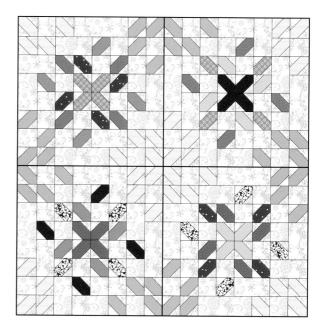

2. Lay out three light-blue print #1 petal units and one 3½" white-and-gray square in two horizontal rows as shown. Sew the pieces in each row together. Press the seam allowances in opposite directions. Sew the rows together. Press the seam allowances in one direction. Repeat to make a total of eight units. Repeat with the light-blue print #2 petal units to make 12 units.

Make 8.

Make 12.

3. Sew a light-blue print #1 petal unit to a 3½"
   white-and-gray square as shown. Press the seam
   allowances toward the square. Repeat to make
   a total of four units. Repeat with the light-blue
   print #2 petal units to make a total of four units.

Make 4 of each.

4. Lay out two light-blue print #1 units from step
   2, two light-blue print #2 units from step 2, one
   light-blue print #1 unit from step 3, one light-
   blue print #2 unit from step 3, and two 6½" x 9½"
   white-and-gray rectangles as shown. Sew the
   pieces together. Press the seam allowances
   as indicated. Repeat to make a total of four
   edge strips.

Make 4.

5. Refer to the quilt assembly diagram on page 81
   to sew edge strips to the top and bottom of the
   quilt center. Press the seam allowances toward
   the edge strips. To the remaining edge strips,
   add a light-blue print #2 unit from step 2 to
   each end as shown. Press the seam allowances
   toward the units from step 2. Sew these strips
   to the sides of the quilt center. The quilt center
   should now measure 60½" x 60½".

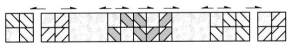

Make 2.

APPLIQUÉING THE MIDDLE BORDER STRIPS

Refer to "Appliqué the Jillily Way" to prepare, position, and stitch the appliqué pieces.

1. Prepare appliqué pieces A–L.

2. Use the 1⅛"-wide light-blue print #1 bias strips
   and the ½" bias-tape maker to make bias tape.
   You'll need eight 21½"-long pieces and sixteen
   3"-long pieces.

3. Sew the 9½" x 42" gray striped strips together
   end to end to make one long strip. From the
   pieced strip, cut two 66½"-long strips and two
   84½"-long strips. Gently press the strips in half
   lengthwise and crosswise to mark the centers.

4. Refer to the appliqué assembly and placement
   diagrams below to position the appliqués on
   the border strips, centering the K pieces. Place
   the 21½"-long bias strips on each side of the
   K pieces and use the 3"-long bias strips for the
   blossom stems. Glue baste the pieces in place
   using Jillily Studio Appli-Glue.

5. Hand or machine stitch the appliqués in place.

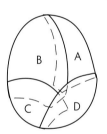

Bud appliqué assembly

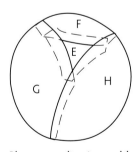

Blossom appliqué assembly

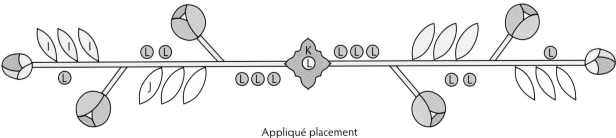

Appliqué placement

ADDING THE BORDERS

1. Sew the 1" x 42" red piping strips together end to end to make one long strip. From the pieced strip, cut four 60½"-long strips. Fold each strip in half lengthwise, wrong sides together, and press to create flat piping.

2. With the raw edges aligned, baste a piping strip to the sides of the quilt center using a ¼" seam allowance. *Do not press the piping away from the quilt center.* Baste the remaining two piping strips to the top and bottom of the quilt center.

3. Sew the 3½" x 42" blue-print strips together end to end to make one long strip. From the pieced strip, cut two 60½"-long strips and two 66½"-long strips for the inner border. Set the remainder of the pieced strip aside for the outer border.

4. Refer to the quilt assembly diagram on page 81 to sew 60½"-long blue-print inner-border strips to the sides of the quilt top, sandwiching the piping between the top and border strip. Press the seam allowances toward the inner border, keeping the piping flat on the quilt center. Sew the 66½"-long blue-print inner-border strips to the top and bottom of the quilt top. Press the seam allowances toward the inner border.

5. Sew the 66½"-long appliquéd border strips to the sides of the quilt top. Press the seam allowances toward the inner border. Sew the 84½"-long appliquéd border strips to the top and bottom of the quilt top. Press the seam allowances toward the inner border.

6. From the remainder of the pieced blue-print strips, cut two 84½"-long strips and two 90½"-long strips for the outer border. Sew the 84½"-long strips to the sides of the quilt top. Press the seam allowances toward the outer border. Sew the 90½"-long strips to the top and bottom of the quilt top. Press the seam allowances toward the outer border.

FINISHING

1. Layer the quilt top with batting and backing. I used bamboo batting in this quilt.

2. Quilt as desired.

3. Bind the edges with the 2¼"x 42" red strips.

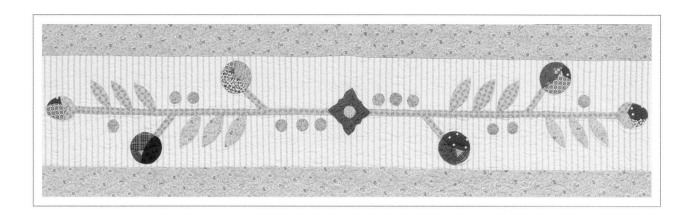

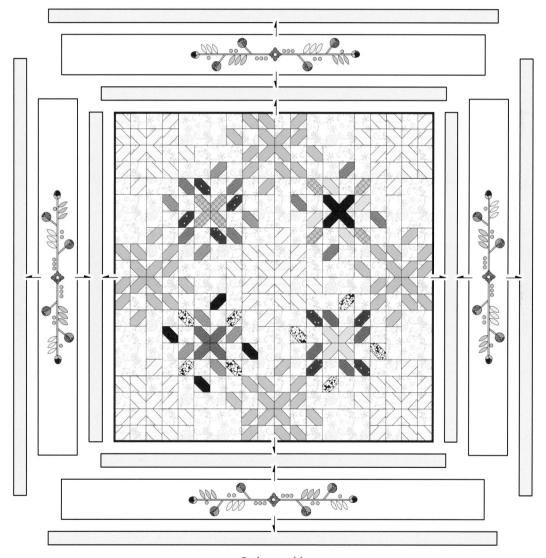

Quilt assembly

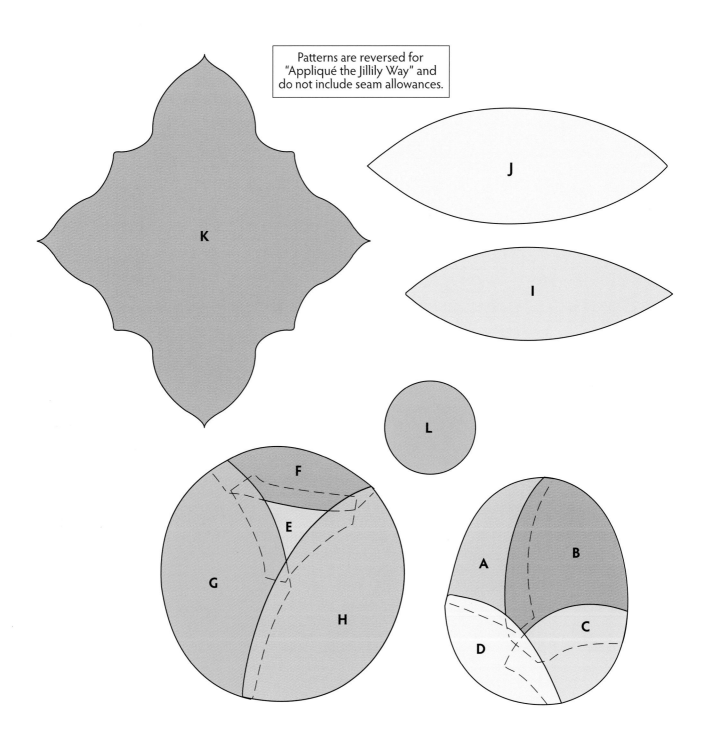

Patterns are reversed for
"Appliqué the Jillily Way" and
do not include seam allowances.

SCATTERED SUNSHINE

Finished quilt size: 88½" x 88½"

Pieced and appliquéd by Jill Finley and Margaret Brockbank; quilted by Virginia Gore

Imagine looking outside through the beveled glass of a leaded window. The scattered sunshine dances across the green landscape, giving you a view of a row of yellow blooms. What a delightful scene to grace your guest bedroom! Who wouldn't feel at home with such a lovely quilt to enjoy? This project has the added bonus of being quick to piece, with a touch of hand appliqué to make it special.

MATERIALS

Yardage is based on 42"-wide fabric.

3⅓ yards of medium-green print for vertical strips

3⅛ yards of white print for vertical strips

2⅛ yards of yellow print for vertical strips and appliqués

⅓ yard *each* of 4 assorted dark-green fabrics for appliqués

8 yards of fabric for backing

96" x 96" square of batting

½" and ¼" bias-tape makers

Freezer paper

Spray starch or sizing

Jillily Studio Appli-Glue (optional)

CUTTING

Refer to "Appliqué the Jillily Way" on page 10 and use patterns A–F on page 88 to make templates for cutting the appliqué pieces.

From the medium-green print, cut:

6 strips, 8½" x 40½"

3 strips, 8½" x 42"; crosscut into 6 strips, 8½" x 20½"

6 strips, 5½" x 42"; crosscut into 42 squares, 5½" x 5½"

From the white print, cut:

5 strips, 8½" x 40½"

5 strips, 8½" x 42"; crosscut into:

    5 rectangles, 8½" x 20½"

    3 rectangles, 8½" x 16½"

    2 squares, 8½" x 8½"

4 strips, 4½" x 42"; crosscut into:

    10 rectangles, 4½" x 8½"

    14 squares, 4½" x 4½"

From the yellow print, cut:

6 strips, 5½" x 42"; crosscut into 42 squares, 5½" x 5½"

2 strips, 4½" x 42"; crosscut into 11 squares, 4½" x 4½"

10 strips, 2¼" x 42"

5 *each* of B and C

10 of F

Continued on page 85.

From the assorted dark-green prints, cut a *total* of:

5 *bias* strips, 1⅛" x approximately 17"
5 pairs of matching *bias* strips, ⅝" x approximately 17"
5 *each* of A, A reversed, D, D reversed, and E

PIECING THE QUILT SECTIONS

1. Draw a diagonal line from corner to corner on the wrong side of each yellow 5½" square. Place a marked square on top of a green 5½" square, right sides together. Sew ¼" from both sides of the marked line. Cut the squares apart on the marked line to make two half-square-triangle units. Press the seam allowances toward the green triangles. Repeat to make a total of 84 half-square-triangle units.

Make 84.

2. Draw a diagonal line from corner to corner and across the seam on the wrong side of 42 half-square-triangle units. Place a marked unit on an unmarked half-square-triangle unit with the colors opposite each other and the seams nested together. Sew ¼" from both sides of the marked line. Cut the units apart on the marked line to make two hourglass units. Repeat to make a total of 84 hourglass units. Trim the units to 4½" x 4½".

Make 84.

Press the seam allowances so they rotate around the center of the unit. To do this, grab the seam allowance at the center of the unit and twist it in the direction of the other seam allowances on the block, splitting the seam at the center. Half of your units will have seam allowances that rotate clockwise and the other

half will have seam allowances that rotate counterclockwise. Keep these groups separated. Trim the units to 4½" x 4½".

3. Using units from the same pressing group, sew 14 hourglass units into pairs, rotating the units as shown and nesting the seams. Sew the pairs together to make a column. Repeat to make six hourglass sections. The sections should measure 8½" x 28½".

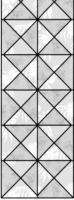

Make 6.

4. Draw a diagonal line from corner to corner on the wrong side of each yellow 4½" square. Place a marked square on top of a white 4½" square, right sides together. Sew on the marked line. Trim ¼" from the stitching line. Press the seam allowances toward the yellow triangle. Repeat to make a total of 10 half-square-triangle units. The units should measure 4½" x 4½". The remaining marked yellow squares will be used in step 6.

Make 10.

5. Sew nine of the half-square-triangle units from step 4 to white 4½" squares to make the three different types of units shown. Press the seam allowances toward the half-square-triangle units. You will not use the remaining unit.

Make 5.   Make 2 of each.

6. Place one of the remaining marked yellow squares on the upper-left corner of a white 8½" x 16½" rectangle as shown, right sides together. Sew on the marked line. Trim ¼" from the stitching line. Press the seam allowances toward the yellow triangle. Repeat on the lower-right corner of the rectangle. Repeat to make a total of three units.

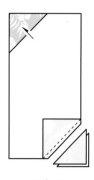

Make 3.

7. Sew white 4½" x 8½" rectangles to the top and bottom of each unit from step 6. Press the seam allowances toward the rectangles.

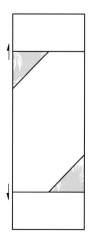

8. Join the units from step 5, the units from step 7, and the white 8½" squares and 4½" x 8½" rectangles to make units A and B. Make three of unit A and two of unit B. The sections should measure 8½" x 28½".

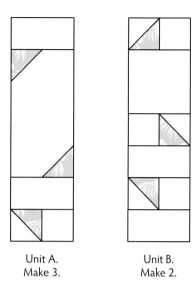

Unit A.   Unit B.
Make 3.   Make 2.

9. Alternately join the green sections from step 3 and the white sections from step 8 to make the pieced center section. Press the seam allowances toward the white sections. The section should measure 88½" x 28½".

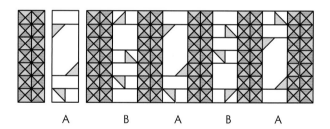

A   B   A   B   A

10. Alternately sew together the green print 8½" x 40½" strips with the white 8½" x 40½" strips to make the bottom section. Because these seams are so long, it's best to use a walking foot or closely pin the sections together to keep the layers from shifting. Press the seam allowances toward the green sections. This section should measure 88½" x 40½".

11. In the same manner, alternately sew together the green and white 8½" x 20½" strips to make the top section. Press the seam allowances toward the green sections. This section should measure 88½" x 20½".

APPLIQUÉING THE BOTTOM SECTION

Refer to "Appliqué the Jillily Way" to prepare, position, and stitch the appliqué pieces.

1. Prepare appliqué pieces A–F.
2. Use the green 1⅛"-wide bias strips and the ½" bias-tape maker to make five bias-tape pieces for the center stems. Trim each stem to 15" long.
3. Use the green ⅝"-wide bias strips and the ¼" bias-tape maker to make five pairs of bias-tape pieces for the side stems. Trim each stem to 15½". Shape each pair of stems so one curves to the left and the other curves to the right as shown in the appliqué placement diagram.
4. Refer to the appliqué placement diagram below to position the center stems, the side stems, and then pieces A–F on the bottom edge of the bottom section. Glue baste the pieces in place using Jillily Studio Appli-Glue.

5. Hand or machine stitch the appliqués in place.
6. Gently press the appliqué section from the wrong side.

ASSEMBLING THE SECTIONS

Sew the top section to the top of the pieced middle section. Add the appliquéd bottom section to the bottom of the pieced middle section. Press the seam allowances toward the top and bottom sections.

FINISHING

1. Layer the quilt top with batting and backing. I used wool batting in this quilt.
2. Quilt as desired.
3. Bind the edges with the yellow 2¼" x 42" strips.

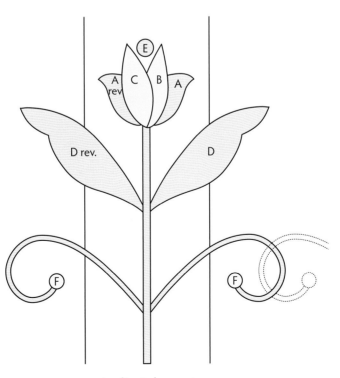

Appliqué placement

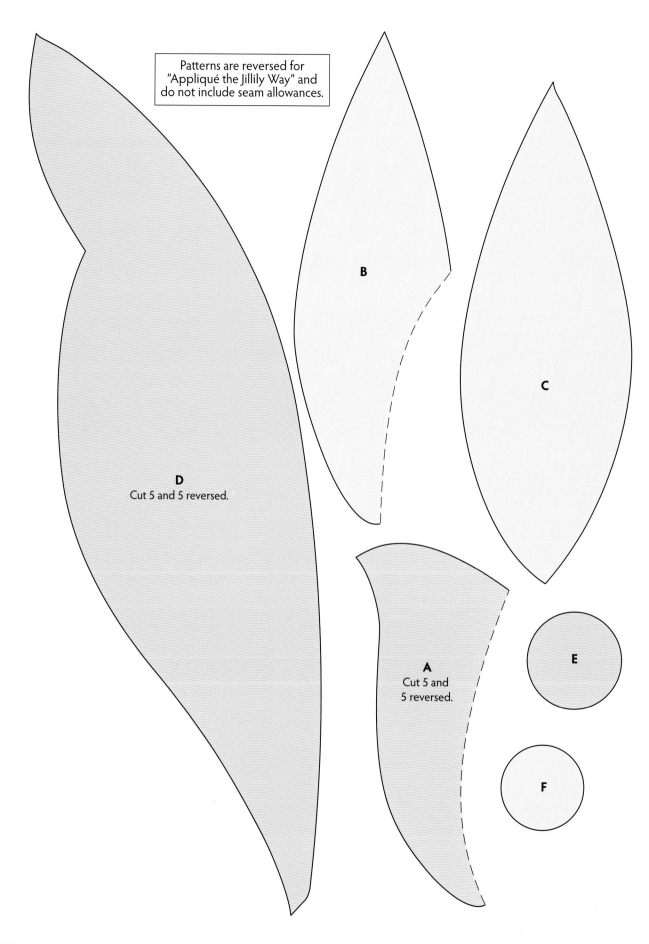

Patterns are reversed for
"Appliqué the Jillily Way" and
do not include seam allowances.

B

C

D
Cut 5 and 5 reversed.

A
Cut 5 and
5 reversed.

E

F

PETAL PUSHERS

Finished quilt size: 52½" x 52½" • Finished block size: 12" x 12"

Pieced and appliquéd by Jill Finley; quilted by Maika Christensen

This quilt is so cute you won't be able to resist it! Gently curved piecing makes this quilt unique and fun. Perfect as a bed topper or a wall hanging, the cheery flowers will brighten any bedroom. The curly vines finish it off with movement and style. Enjoy this fun little quilt!

MATERIALS
Yardage is based on 42"-wide fabric.

2⅝ yards of white print for blocks and borders

2 yards of pink print for blocks and binding

1⅛ yards of green print for appliqués and outer border

3¼ yards of fabric for backing

58" x 58" square of batting

⅜" bias-tape maker

Freezer paper

Spray starch or sizing

Jillily Studio Appli-Glue (optional)

CUTTING
Refer to "Appliqué the Jillily Way" on page 10 and use patterns A and B on pages 93 and 94 to make templates for cutting the piecing shapes, and the circle pattern on page 94 for cutting the appliqué pieces. Transfer the alignment dots from the A and B templates to each fabric piece.

From the white print, cut:
5 strips, 6½" x 42"; trim *2 of the strips* to 6½" x 36½"

40 of B

16 of A

From the pink print, cut:
32 of B

20 of A

6 strips, 2¼" x 42"

From the green print, cut:
1 strip, 18" x 42"; cut 10 *bias* strips, ⅞" x approximately 25"

6 strips, 2½" x 42"

5 of C

PIECING THE BLOCKS

1. Place a white B piece on top of a pink A piece, right sides together. Match the center dot and pin in place. Now, match the outside dots of each piece, and pin. Gently ease the remainder of the curves together, matching the raw edges and pinning in place.

2. Stitch ¼" from the pinned edge along the seam line, pulling out each pin just before you reach it. As you stitch, watch the A fabric to be sure it doesn't shift. Guide and straighten both pieces of fabric as you stitch.

3. Repeat steps 1 and 2 to add a second white B piece to the opposite side of the pink A piece to make a pink petal unit. Press the seam allowances toward the A piece. The unit should measure 6½" x 6½".

4. Repeat steps 1–3 with the remaining pink A pieces and white B pieces to make a total of 20 pink petal units, and with the white A pieces and pink B pieces to make a total of 16 white petal units.

Make 20.

Make 16.

5. Lay out four pink petal units in two rows of two units each as shown. Sew the units in each row together. Press the seam allowances in each row in opposite directions. Sew the rows together. Press the seam allowances toward the top of the block. Repeat to make a total of five pink blocks. Repeat with the white petal units to make four white blocks, pressing the seam allowances toward the bottom of the block.

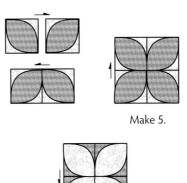
Make 5.

Make 4.

ASSEMBLING THE QUILT TOP

1. Refer to the quilt assembly diagram on page 92 to lay out the blocks in three rows of three blocks each, alternating the pink and white blocks in each row and from row to row. Sew the blocks in each row together. Press the seam allowances in opposite directions from row to row. Sew the rows together. Press the seam allowances in one direction. The quilt center should measure 36½" x 36½".

2. Sew the white 6½" x 36½" inner-border strips to the sides of the quilt center. Press the seam allowances toward the border strips. Sew the remaining three white 6½" x 42" strips together end to end to make one long strip. From the pieced strip, cut two 48½"-long strips. Sew these strips to the top and bottom of the quilt top. Press the seam allowances toward the border strips.

3. Sew the green 2½" x 42" outer-border strips together end to end to make one long strip. From the pieced strip, cut two 48½"-long strips and two 52½"-long strips. Sew the 48½"-long strips to the sides of the quilt top. Press the seam allowances toward the outer border. Sew the 52½"-long strips to the top and bottom of the quilt center. Press the seam allowances toward the outer border.

APPLIQUÉING THE QUILT

Refer to "Appliqué the Jillily Way" to prepare, position, and stitch the appliqué pieces.

1. Prepare the appliqué C pieces. Glue baste a C piece to the center of each pink flower block using Jillily Studio Appli-Glue.

2. Use the ⅞"-wide bias strips and the bias-tape maker to make 10 bias-tape pieces. Referring to the quilt photo on page 89, use the bias-tape pieces to create two vines on each pink flower. Shape the vines into curves and loops as shown in the photo, trimming as necessary. Carefully undo just enough of the seam where each vine meets the petals to stick the end of the vine into the seam. Hand stitch the opening closed. Turn the other end of the vine under, and glue baste in place.

3. Hand or machine stitch the appliqués in place.

FINISHING

1. Layer the quilt top with batting and backing. I used 100% cotton batting in this quilt.

2. Quilt as desired.

3. Bind the edges with the pink 2¼" x 42" strips.

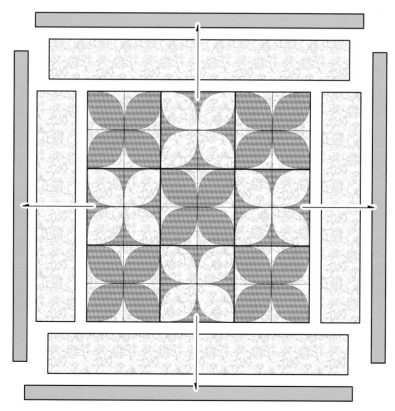

Quilt assembly

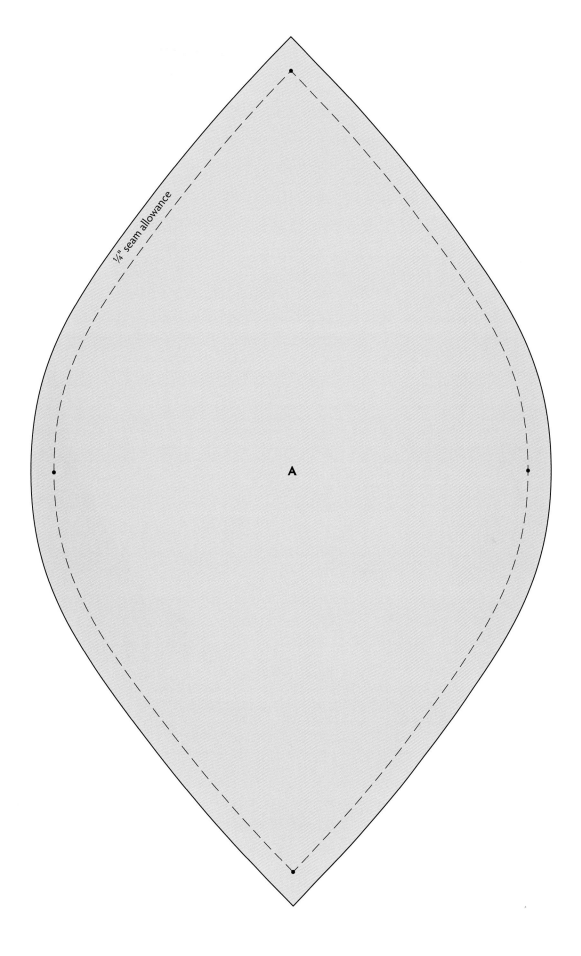

¼" seam allowance

A

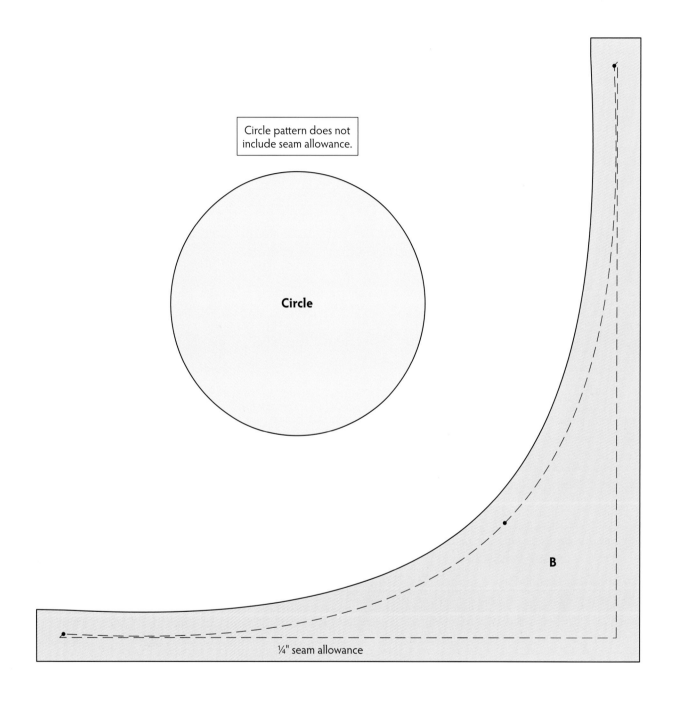

Circle pattern does not
include seam allowance.

Circle

B

¼" seam allowance

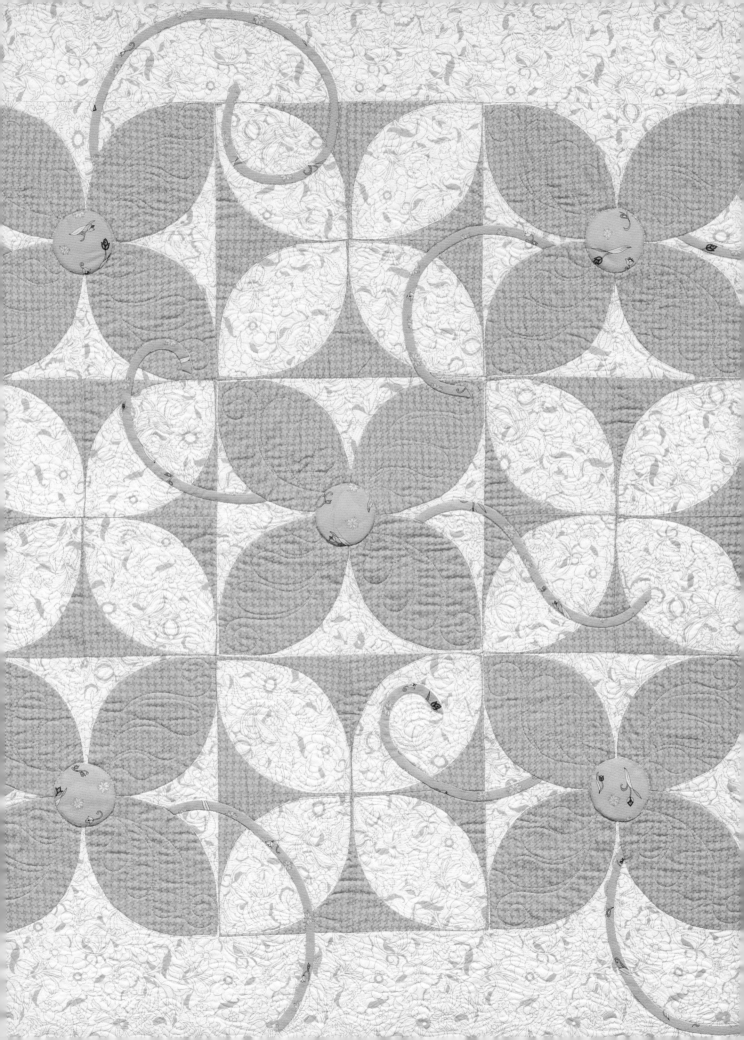

ABOUT THE AUTHOR

Jill Finley has been designing quilt patterns for more than 15 years. Her creative spirit and affinity for working with fabrics result in a fresh take on traditional quiltmaking. She has an eye for color and pattern and loves to add the soft curves of appliqué to finish many of her quilts.

In 2007 Jill launched her design business, Jillily Studio, through which she designs and sells quilt patterns, fabrics, kits, and notions. Her designs have been featured in several magazines, including *American Patchwork and Quilting, Quilt,* and *Quilter's Home.*

Jill says she's inspired by many quilting friends and family. She teaches and lectures at shops and guilds across the country. "I love to share the joy and satisfaction that I get from playing with fabric with anyone who is interested. Sometimes even if they aren't!"

Jill has developed a line of notions that includes Jillily Studio Appli-Glue, an archival-quality basting glue for use in appliqué, and Jillily Studio Poke-A-Dots, which are small, sticky thimbles to protect your fingers when hand sewing. She hopes to bring many more notions to the quilting world in the future.

While Jill stays busy filling orders for patterns, notions, and kits, she still makes time for new designs. Creating fabric designs for Henry Glass and Company has been one of her favorite projects. She's working on her sixth fabric line and is so happy to see their success so far. "It is great to see my designs actually become fabric. I love what I do. It is a joy to be able to create new designs and have others enjoy them too." Many of the quilts in this book feature Jill's fabrics. She also carries kits for many of the projects.

Jill loves to spend time with her family—working, playing, reading, gardening, sewing, cooking, and learning. She and her husband, Randy, live in Utah, surrounded by the beautiful scenery of the nearby mountains and canyons. They're the parents of seven children and are blessed with six grandchildren. There's always a party of some kind going on at the Finley home. It's a happy life!

Follow Jill online at jillilystudio.com.